WE PREPARE AND PREACH

WE PREPARE AND PREACH

The Practice of Sermon Construction and Delivery

Edited by

CLARENCE STONELYNN RODDY, Ph.D.,

Professor of Homiletics and Practical Theology,
Fuller Theological Seminary,
Pasadena, California

MOODY PRESS

CHICAGO

Printed in the United States of America

Introduction

PREACHING IS A GREAT SUBJECT! Is there a greater? Homiletics because of its involvement with preaching becomes in itself a great subject. Any word that can help men preach the glorious Gospel of Jesus Christ has its validation within itself. Furthermore, homiletics is a live subject. While its basic principles do not change, their application is conditioned by the temper and pulse of the generation to which the preacher interprets and witnesses. There is need, therefore, for new expressions of its spirit and its body as the Gospel is presented to this day. Certainly homiletics cannot enshroud itself in the concept "that no more needs to be said," but must continue to grow as John Stuart Mill expressed it: "On all great subjects much remains to be said."

These studies in the attempt to reduce the area of the "much that remains," depart from the formal type of text. They present the methods of eleven outstanding preachers in the evangelical position. In these articles we find a common depth of conviction as to the sacredness of the call of the preacher and of the cardinal truths of the Christian faith, rooted and grounded in that conviction which gives power and character to preaching, namely, the belief that the Bible is the inspired Word of God. In personality and method and manner of expression the contributors differ. In adherence to the basic principles of homiletics they are one.

This volume does not attempt to supplant normal texts, but rather to supplement. While books such as those by Broadus and Blackwood, and lectures by Brooks and Jowett are staple diet, the examples of the men presented will help other prophets to *hammer out their own particular method* on the anvil of everyday experience. In most fields it is customary to study the techniques and methods of those who have proved themselves efficient and effective. This we attempt by presenting the art and skills of proved masters. One often wonders how men so involved in the intricacies of modern churchcraft and plunged so deeply into the maelstrom of the pressures and tensions of modern society maintain such a high standard of pulpit excellence. Here they share their secrets. Here they speak not from the towers of academic cloisters but from the throbbing, pulsating forum of life.

We believe that the student, the young pastor, the man who has never had formal training in homiletics, even the mature preacher, in fact, anyone interested in presenting the Gospel, will find this volume both a service and an inspiration.

We express our appreciation to the busy men of God who have made possible this study.

—CLARENCE S. RODDY

Contents

Introduction 5

WILLIAM WARD AYER

My Method of Preparation......................... 9
The Holy Spirit and Daily Living.................. 18

DONALD GREY BARNHOUSE

On Expository Preaching.......................... 29
Living from the Word of God...................... 37

HOWARD W. FERRIN

A Distinctive Style................................ 45
The True Teachers................................ 53

J. LESTER HARNISH

The Mechanics Employed.......................... 63
Your Greatest Privilege........................... 71

ROBERT G. LEE

Forty-Seven Years................................ 80
Christ Above All.................................. 86

J. VERNON McGEE

The Pulpit and the Well of Life.................... 98
The Human Story.................................104

HAROLD JOHN OCKENGA

A Hard Lesson to Learn...........................113
Dr. Luke Testifies of Physical Resurrection.............122

7

ALAN REDPATH

Five Principles of Sermon Preparation.................134
The Art of Winning a Soul for Jesus..................138

PAUL STROMBERG REES

A Sermon Is Born....................................145
The Drama of Double Search.........................149

WILBUR MOOREHEAD SMITH

No Set Rules..160
Life—Through Jesus Christ..........................169

J. R. W. STOTT

Stewards of God....................................179
The Exaltation of Jesus............................185

WILLIAM WARD AYER

Born in Shediac, New Brunswick, Canada, of American parents, came to New York when twelve years of age. Converted in the "Billy" Sunday Campaign, Boston.

Moody Bible Institute, Lincoln College, and Northern Baptist Seminary; honorary D.D. from Bob Jones University.

Pastor, First Baptist Church, Valparaiso, Indiana, 1922-27; Central Baptist Church, Gary, Indiana, 1927-32; Philpott Tabernacle, Hamilton, Ontario, 1932-36; Calvary Baptist Church, New York City, 1936-50; trustee, Eastern Baptist Seminary, Bob Jones University; Member of the Board, American Leprosy Missions, and North Africa Mission Council.

Author: *Seven Saved Sinners; God's Answers to Man's Doubts; Flame for the Altar; The Christian, His Bible and War;* and others.

In Radio and Evangelistic work.

Broadcaster, Evangelist, Author, and Teacher.

My Method of Preparation

I HAVE BEEN ASKED to give my method of sermon preparation; I hesitate to do so because I fear that too many times my method has been quite haphazard. If I ever have preached well, it is from a full mind and a warm heart. These two things are necessary.

The sermon normally begins when the minister devotionally reads his Bible. In the feeding of his own soul he finds material with which to feed others. Theological students have been warned against a type of topical preaching that

9

takes a text as a pretext or a point of departure, while the pulpiteer presents his ideas on some public question or Christian doctrine. The best sermons are created when the text primarily chooses the man, and not the man the text.

It has been my procedure to put down in a large loose-leaf book text and thought that impressed me, then make a tentative outline and development. I have filled several letter-size loose-leaf binders with sermonic ideas which were born in moments of inspiration, in reading the Bible and in reading Christian literature. Often I have consolidated many of these thoughts and discovered I had the makings of instructive messages. The facts, of course, needed to be marshaled, properly illustrated, and the fire rekindled for pulpit ministries.

I started early in my ministry to clip and file magazine reading, using the *Wilson's Topical and Textual Index System.* It is alphabetically arranged and has a very satisfactory tab system for the topics and subtopics. Thousands of clippings were filed away in appropriate classified and numbered folders. Their topics and locations were registered in the *Topical Index Book.*

I also use the Wilson Index in cataloguing most of my library, according to texts, topics, doctrines, etc. For that I needed to register by books and catalogue them according to the subject and number of their registration. Then in my reading I recorded in the index important material that has been referred to again and again for sermon making.

In later years, I have been too busy to do too much of this, so I have resorted to the less adequate, easier method of filling drawers of filing cabinets with material on subjects, giving a library of clippings with immediate access to a wealth of material on major topics and texts. I can almost at a moment's notice have material before me which can be marshaled for perhaps a dozen messages.

My library is not filled with too many sets of sermonic volumes. At the beginning of my ministry I avoided the use of pulpit commentaries with their wealth of ready-made outlines because I feared they might become crutches upon which to lean too heavily. Because my outlines have been my own, I think they have been more effective in the preaching.

C. H. M.'s Notes (on the Pentateuch, six vols.), the expositions of Alexander Maclaren have been a blessing from the early days of my ministry. Dr. W. B. Riley's volumes on *The Bible of the Expositor and the Evangelist* have given me much illustrative material. Here and there they have supplied a unique approach to some Biblical theme. *The Homiletic Commentary* has been referred to and some scholarly thoughts have been given me. *Parker's Expositions* have been a mental stimulant, but yielded little that was usable for my congregations. Spurgeon's *Treasury of David* has been a great help when I have preached from the Psalms. The several volumes of *The Biblical Commentary on the Old Testament,* which is the work of the bishops and others of the Anglican Church, edited by F. C. Cook, Canon of Exeter, is both scholarly and practical. Although there are many other sets of commentaries these are the ones I use the most.

The four-volume encyclopedia, *Dictionary of Christ and the Gospels* and *Dictionary of the Apostolic Church,* has been of the utmost value to me in my study, as of course has been the invaluable *International Standard Bible Encyclopaedia.*

For commentaries on the books of the Bible I have shelves of one-volume and multiple-volume up-to-date commentaries; much more usable and practical in the main than the older commentaries.

Profitable for my own study and for my congregations are the preparation and delivery of series of sermons on Biblical characters, Bible questions, great doctrines, practical Christian responsibilities. One series was published in book form, *These Men Live* (Bible characters); another was *Questions*

Jesus Answered; and the third, *Marked Men* which deals with the marks of discipleship, the hypocrite, the religious traitor, the soul-winner, the Pharisee, the mature Christian, the patriot, the Mark of the Beast, and the marks of Christ. Preaching series of sermons I found ties the people closer to the preaching ministry. A series encourages faithfulness to every service, and eliminates the hectic and frantic attitude of the preacher who wails: "What shall I preach on next Sunday?" It avoids wasting time casting about here and there for an idea.

I have usually planned my preaching ministry months ahead, leaving room, of course, for thoughts and ideas and responsibilities which the Spirit may place upon me.

I am often asked how long it takes to prepare a sermon. Some sermons have taken twenty years. They have been in my mind, and some thoughts have been on paper that long before the occasion made me choose the message or the message chose me for its preaching.

During my fourteen-year pastorate at Calvary Baptist Church, in New York, where time for everything was "of the essence," my usual routine was to have a conference with the whole church staff on Tuesday morning, then immediately go to work on my messages for Sunday morning, evening, and the midweek service, together with any other special meetings that I might have.

If preaching a series of sermons, I would choose divisions of the subject, roughly outline those divisions to make sure that every phase of the subject was covered and that there would be as little duplication as possible from message to message. These subjects were advertised in the church calendar weeks, sometimes months, in advance. After several hours of this work, all of the material was placed in a folder and frequently not touched again until Thursday, except for the Wednesday night study which normally would be handled on Wednesday afternoon. The business and the detail of church work (a church with a budget of a quarter of a million dollars) would have to be handled; so it was not possible to give time every day to sermon preparation.

Wednesday night (midweek service) brought a multitude of obligations—meetings with the deacons, counseling with candidates for church membership, often meeting with other committees; then the Bible-teaching service where even in normal times six or seven hundred people met together to study some book of the Bible.

During that time I was living in Scarsdale (25 miles away from the church), and whenever possible I stayed at home on Thursday with books and pamphlets and commentaries which I would take from my church study. A good part of Thursday was spent putting the finishing touches on the messages. Previous to that I had written a résumé of the sermon for the newspapers. *The New York Times* and *Herald-Tribune* were very generous in giving space through the major portion of my ministry. I wrote my copy and submitted it to the newspapers early in the week.

On Thursday the messages were completely outlined and reference books and other material to be studied and digested were noted. On Friday morning one of my secretaries typed the notes. Nothing further was done about them until Saturday night at home in my den. There those notes would be gone over, the references studied, the message bathed in prayer for God's blessing upon it. Sunday morning I gave the notes a brief going over to refresh my mind before I went into the pulpit. The same procedure was followed late Sunday afternoon for the evening message.

I believe in thorough preparation for pulpit ministries. Of course, I have not always performed what I believe. But I also believe that too much preparation, that is, the sort of preparation that brings what we might call a "finished product" to the pulpit, is injurious to powerful preaching.

If the fire burns more brightly in the study than it does

in the pulpit, the congregation has missed the best of the preacher. Let the study be the place where the material for the pulpit fire is gathered and arranged, where zeal is created, but see to it that the fire blazes in the pulpit as the minister preaches. In the study the preacher must build the altar and put the wood in place, then on the Lord's Day lay the sacrifice on the altar. When the preacher stands in the pulpit let him ask God to let the fire fall and consume the sacrifice, and the people will know that their preacher is a burning light as well as a shining one. Many earnest preachers are so zealous for literary perfection in the delivery of their sermons that they burn everything up in the study, and carry a pan of ashes into the pulpit.

In my early ministry I tried, on a majority of occasions, to preach without notes. However, I made the outline and memorized it, also memorized the illustrations. This "extemporaneous" style had a challenging effect upon the congregation. I was not tied to notes and, except for times when it took me a second or two to remember what came next, I had a liberty that is not always present when one is tied too closely to notes.

In later years the increase in responsibility forbade that. I found my mind at ease when the subject on which I was to speak was well documented in notes before me, although I did not follow them exactly as the message was given.

If notes are used, the speaker should not be burdened with a sense of dependence upon them. God rarely fills the mouth of an unprepared man; but He does often, in the pulpit, illumine the mind with potent thoughts which would never arise in the quiet atmosphere of the study.

There is a sense in which the pulpit is a battleground. If the preacher is really "in the Spirit" there are times in preaching when he is conscious of forces of Hell arrayed against him—principalities and powers in the heavenlies—ever present to challenge the most powerful thing in the universe, the preaching of the Word of God. The preacher should use notes only as running shoes to speed the spiritual progress of the message, not as crutches to impede it.

We all recall that one of the supreme tributes paid to Jesus' preaching was that He "spake as one having authority and not as the scribes." The philosophic, sometimes apologetic, mild approach of many a modern preacher is very pleasing to a congregation which likes to spend a dreamy hour in a religious Lotus Land. Suaveness and sweet amiability in the presentation of the pulpit message is a good deal like Niagara River several miles back from the Falls—beautiful to look upon, but without power. Only when the river pours itself as a roaring torrent to the chasm below is there creative power. I do not recommend a roaring torrent of noise for the preacher; I do recommend power that is generated by a deep sense of authority. There should be authority in tone and bearing, not an assumed authority but a real one—an authority based on the knowledge of the eternal truth of the message, a feeling that the messenger is standing in Christ's stead bidding men to be reconciled to God.

It takes real insight to see the difference between authority and "cockiness." The latter is an abomination, but the apologetic preacher never yet influenced people for God. Holy boldness probably is the name of the desired quality, and the Holy Spirit creates a proper boldness in the preacher. He clothes manliness and virility in the soft garments of humility.

The preacher must so prepare himself that there is liberty in the delivery of the sermon. Liberty is a supernatural thing—it is the work of the Spirit. It is liberty of thought, of speech, of spiritual zeal and power. There are times when the preacher should feel like I think Samson felt when the power of God came upon him and he grabbed the ass's jawbone, backed into a corner and yelled for the Philistines to come on.

Eloquence in pulpit speech is not as predominant as it used to be, except perhaps in some sections of the Southland. Human eloquence is a bouquet of fading flowers, but the eloquence of a divine passion means the outpouring of torrents of truth through lips of clay. Human eloquence is like a painted fire: it will not long attract for it has no warmth in it. Uninspired eloquence is like the cotton candy you buy at the circus—squeeze it and all you have is a small residue of pink sugar in the palm of your hand.

Above all there must be earnest and genuine spiritual enthusiasm. The preacher must be possessed by the message. Some preaching is like an old mother hen pecking and clucking. She finds a grain of corn, breaks it with her bill, and then gives small portions to her brood. The food has never become a part of her. She just cuts and distributes what she has found.

I am not facetious when I say that much preaching is like that. It is the taking of a few attractive verses of Scripture and giving a dissertation upon them with a good deal of "clucking." The message may be orthodox, practical, and helpful, but it is obvious that the preacher is giving something that has never become a part of him. In this lies its ineffectiveness.

In contradistinction I would present as an example old "Bossy" who feeds her calf that which she has first eaten, digested, and providentially turned into rich milk. In other words, she gives of herself. How much more effective much of today's preaching would be if the Word that is given forth had first richly dwelt in the preacher, if he had entered into the experience, and could speak out of a warmed heart by his fellowship with God! If only he could say with the disciples, "I speak what I do know"!

Now to the man behind the message: John tells us that "the Word was made flesh"; so it is in preaching, the Word must be made to live, before it is effective. Nothing is more effective than personal conviction. God still speaks out of "the bush that burns with fire." This is the first requisite of the man behind the message. Conviction is born of genuine Christian experience, a personal and vivid knowledge of the grace of God. We often censure preachers because they are not evangelistic; they can never be evangelistic because they have never had that experience which is a prerequisite to an evangelistic ministry.

The man behind the message must live a life that is in keeping with the demands of the Gospel. He must have a right vision of the world and a right philosophy concerning the Gospel. The preacher must see the world as lost and the Gospel as its only salvation. If he has accepted an evolutionary philosophy and believes that the world is slowly but surely "by means of resident forces and according to fixed laws" evolving toward some sort of perfection and all that he can do is give it a little nudge in its upward trend, he certainly is not likely to be very strong and Biblical in his pulpit ministry.

The man behind the sermon must look at the world not merely as a world poor, sick, and deluded, but as a world at enmity with, and under the wrath of, God. He must not ally himself with it or expect anything but enmity, either passive or active, from it. While the minister has many other things to do in his preaching, basically he must warn men to flee from the wrath to come, and in the spirit of Isaiah must say: "Woe is me! . . . because I am a man of unclean lips . . . for mine eyes have seen the King, the Lord of hosts."

The Holy Spirit and Daily Living

William Ward Ayer

When he, the Spirit of truth, is come, he shall guide you into all the truth, for he shall not speak from himself. . . . He shall glorify me; for he shall take of mine, and shall declare it unto you—John 16:13, 14 (A.S.V.).

THERE IS A NEWFANGLED RELIGION sweeping the land. Millions are flocking to it. It is not another church or denomination—you do not have to leave your own church to follow the new creed. It is a sort of rider on the religious insurance policy you already have.

This new religion is popular. Basically, it is simple—oversimplified; but it has strong appeal. Why, it is full of magic! It feeds carnal desires, matches boasted achievements. It is a "Religious Success Story." Things folk want to happen, really happen, is the claim.

You see, the old-time responsibilities and dogged hill climbing that have been a part of Christian experience since the days of the apostles are not necessary any more.

What is this new cult? It has been aptly called "The Cult of Reassurance," and it seems to be beneficial to many. Its premises are tremendous. It preaches that if you expect the best in life you will get it. He who thinks he can, *can!*

The new religious philosophy promises to heal almost everything that is wrong: your mental attitudes, your economic difficulties, your worries and defeats. Not only that, but your body prospers and your general appearance is enhanced.

Of course, the new cult recommends that God be called into the picture in the process, but really God is not fully necessary—it is the *formula* that works the miracle. Christ and His redemptive work for man is scarcely mentioned, and the Holy Spirit and His regenerating power is forgotten.

What is this cult? It is a sort of religious tranquilizer which keeps its adherents from facing life's problems.

Can we massage out of existence the cancer of sin? Can we create godly character without the new birth and Christ's indwelling? Need sinful man any longer get low before God and like Job say, "repent in sackcloth and ashes"? Have we really turned a corner in the progress of religion, and has psychiatry and modern medicine eliminated the phobias of modern living?

Fear grips the hearts of people today. Like drowning men they will grasp anything that promises to keep them afloat in a world where a sudden tidal wave of atomic war may sink civilization and all its boasted achievements. But why forsake the strong and safe "gospel ship" for the floating debris of men's popular philosophies?

WORRYLESS

Think! Jesus never said Christian living would be easy, worryless, popular, successful. To the contrary He warned, "In this world ye shall have tribulation."

"There is nothing to fear but fear itself" is an overworked slogan, basically a lie. Jesus said there was plenty to fear but that God could overcome fear for those who put their trust in His omnipotence. "Fear not, I have overcome the world," He said.

The new religious philosophy is a sort of "save a life, especially your own" proposition. Jesus said: "Whosoever shall save his life shall lose it; and whosoever shall lose his life for my sake and the gospel's, the same shall save it."

There's a sad awakening ahead for those who try to live by a faith that takes no account of defeats and heartbreaks. The new cult does not prepare folk to trust God in the shadows, remembering "though He may send some affliction, 'twill but make me long for Home" and "though I walk through the valley of the shadow of death, I will fear no evil."

This Pollyanna philosophy is sweet but not sound. To be a Christian is not to be delivered from all trouble. Heaven has no vaccine that immunizes us from life's vexatious problems. Some of God's saints have been immersed in trouble and have grown in grace as they appropriated God's promise, "I will be with him in trouble." Even our Lord was not immunized: "Though he were a Son, yet learned he obedience by the things which he suffered." God's people need ever to be conscious of Christ's indwelling presence by the Holy Spirit. The Holy Spirit creates within us a solid faith. The early Christians were constantly victorious even though they had little and suffered much.

Paul told the persecuted Philippian Christians to "rejoice in the Lord alway: and again I say, Rejoice. Let your forbearance be known unto all men. The Lord is at hand. Be careful for nothing; but in everything by prayer and supplication with thanksgiving let your requests be made known unto God. And the peace of God, which passeth all understanding, shall guard your hearts and your thoughts in Christ Jesus" (A.S.V.).

FREE

We live under the law of the "Spirit of life in Christ Jesus which has made us free from the law of sin and death." When we were dead in sin, the Holy Spirit made us alive. The Christian life is a Spirit-led life: "For as many as are led by the Spirit of God, these are sons of God" (Rom. 8:14, A.S.V.).

There can be no real Christian living where God's Holy Spirit is ignored. The presence of the Holy Spirit helps rid us of our fears and worries. Let us face facts. With Christ operative within we do not fear, for love dwells in us. And there is no fear in love, for perfect love casteth out fear!

Let me, however, warn you that the Spirit's presence does not permit an indifferent dodging of issues. God's people cannot deny the existence of evil without making themselves deluded people. The new religion says, "Believe in yourself"; the Spirit says, "Believe on Christ and crucify yourself."

Galatians 5:22, 23 (A.S.V.) reveals that the indwelling Holy Spirit produces a new character within the believer: "The fruit of the Spirit is love, joy, peace, longsuffering, kindness, goodness, faithfulness, meekness, self-control. . . ." Christian character is not therefore developed by following a life philosophy, but it is a supernatural creation within the human heart.

It is a life of self-forgetfulness. True Christians help others and forget themselves, which is one of the best ways of getting rid of neuroses.

The Christian is to "bear one another's burdens and thus fulfill the law of Christ." In all this "cult of reassurance" there is too much looking after one's own welfare. Little is done for other people because we just cannot ruffle our serene personalities by assuming responsibility for the troubles of others.

Some years ago I counseled with a neurotic woman in New York. For nearly an hour she poured out her woes, troubles, frustrations, and disappointments. Obviously she really had nothing wrong with her physically; and her troubles were no worse than those of the average person who goes on through life courageously, braving the storms, breasting the waves, and coming out on top of bad situations. She said to me, "Pastor, what shall I do? Give me some advice."

She did not like the advice I gave her. I said, "Get out of your home, forget your personal troubles, and start helping others who are in real trouble, and you will soon forget about your own problems. Remember Christ; He had many troubles but He forgot Himself into immortality."

No Cure

But the dear woman was indignant. How could a minister make a suggestion like that! She froze me with a disgusted stare, and I left her. But my prescription would have cured her. The fact is, she did not want a cure—she really enjoyed her troubles by seeking sympathy.

It is strange that most of us are willing to live under tyrants. Some accept the tyranny of pain and trouble. They would rather suffer them and constantly complain than let Christ lift them above them. Some live under the tyranny of temper, driven sometimes to frenzy by its lashings. Some live under the tyranny of drink—alcohol destroys them and they know it. Yet they scarcely protest. Many are tyrannized by the little vexatious things of life. They protest against them but never lift a hand to destroy them.

The Holy Spirit in us will deliver us from this tyranny if we are yielded. Christianity leads to freedom: "If the Son shall make you free, you shall be free indeed." "Walk in the Spirit and ye shall not fulfill the desires of the flesh."

The worldling sympathetically looks at the Christian and says, "Poor fellow, he's behind prison bars. His life is sad and drab—but I have freedom!" What delusion!

In reality no man is free until Christ makes him free. God's child knows a freedom, not dependent on the Bill of Rights, but the inner liberty of God's Spirit. "Christ has delivered us from the curse of the law." Christ delivers from Satan's tyranny, for Christ defeated the Devil at the cross.

Christ has also delivered us from the law of sin and death
Let us not be subject to tyrants!

The procedure for the Spirit's operation is given in Philippians 4:8, 9: "Whatsoever things are true, whatsoever things are honest . . . just . . . pure . . . lovely . . . if there be any virtue, and if there be any praise, think on these things . . . and the peace of God shall be with you."

OUR NEEDS

The Gospel declares that evil is real and that Jesus dealt with it, but good is greater than evil. One of our needs as orthodox Christians is a sane and happy outlook on life, because there is evil everywhere. It is a prophesied fulfillment which sometimes makes the believer so sad. Yet the Spirit-guided believer goes on in peace knowing that in whatsoever state he finds himself he is content (Phil. 4:11).

A Christian asked a friend how he was getting along. Dolefully his friend replied, "Oh, fairly well, under the circumstances."

"I am sorry," the Christian replied, "that you are under the circumstances. The Lord would have us living above all circumstances, where He Himself can satisfy our hearts and meet our every need for time and eternity."

I have seen people get so holy they become sloppy. Do not be forever looking for evil. Sickness and self-centeredness often go together.

A prominent missionary tells how he visited a sanitarium where people were recovering from a disease. He asked some who had nothing to do to sew and knit for China, which was then accessible and known as the "continent of pain" because of so much poverty and suffering.

These sick people had so many hours on their hands they did not know what to do with them. The missionary thought they would be glad to do something for the unfortunate and would crowd upon the lady he designated to provide them simple work as they whiled away the hours while their bodies were mending.

To his surprise not one person volunteered, and he saw for the first time that sickness and self-centeredness often go hand in hand. People become so interested in their own well-being that they lack interest in the suffering of others. I wonder if that does not explain the tremendous crowds that are now waiting upon the so-called "divine healers" who seem more interested in the temporary aches and pains of people than in getting them saved eternally.

Christianity is really a continuously saving experience. It is a process of development toward Christlikeness. We are not finished products at the beginning. There are too many illusions of grandeur among Christians. They boast that they have been saved and that they are now children of God, and all they have is an initial experience. Unfortunately they try to measure others by their own standards.

Set Goals

Do not belittle yourself, or expect the impossible of yourself. Set goals you can attain. I have had to face that in the ministry many times. I have worked long hours and at the end of the week felt I had not accomplished one-third of what I planned. I left my study frustrated with a sense of defeat. I had to learn to map out a program I could reasonably achieve and then there was a sense of achievement and happiness.

My father was a harsh disciplinarian and hard worker. He expected every one of the family to work as hard as he. During the summer vacation he would go off to work and lay out for me a set of tasks which no boy could do in one day even if he worked himself, as I often did, into a frenzy. Then when the job was not done he would whip me. Eventually I became fatalistic. I did what I could and went off fishing because I knew a whipping was coming anyway. Something happened to me then that has been hard to overcome in the succeeding years.

Remember, with God all things are possible, but with you many things are impossible. You are just a developing saint —you have not arrived! Watch against defeat when trials and difficulties come—and they will come for we are in the process of development and God uses these things to shape us into saints.

When trouble comes we cannot flee from it, nor can we always fight it. The indwelling Spirit tells us: "Our wrestling is not against flesh and blood, but against the principalities, against the powers, against the world-rulers of this darkness, against the spiritual hosts of wickedness in the heavenly places." Of course, we have to fight the good fight of faith, but when we start fighting our troubles we discover they are too numerous. It is like fighting a swarm of bees. We just cannot win.

The Christian way is to face up to our troubles. God often gives us strength so that if we really face our problems squarely, He can give us great victory. Often Satan exaggerates our troubles and we fear our weak human nature will faint when sorrows fall like rain. But when we face difficulties and make a minute examination of the things that distress us, it is usually revealed that they are greatly inflated.

Another thing, do not make too much demand upon other people. One of the sins of Christian people is that they make more demands upon others than they do upon themselves. Many are continuously unhappy because they see shortcomings in other people. We had better overlook them and look more at our own failures. It is strange how readily we make stern and exacting demands upon others and not upon ourselves. I heard of a woman who fired her maid for "stealing my priceless . . . [a well-known hotel name] towels."

FAILURES

The cure is this: Let the Holy Spirit turn thoughts away
from self to Christ. Remember what Christ told His disciples (John 16:13, 14, A.S.V.) : "When he, the Spirit of truth,
is come, he shall guide you into all the truth: for he shall not
speak from himself; but what things soever he shall hear,
these shall he speak . . . he shall glorify me: for he shall take
of mine, and shall declare it unto you."

Look away to Jesus. Look away from aches and pains, sins
and failures. No use stirring up the "mud" of your personality. Do not half live, like a car with its engine hitting on
half the cylinders. Do not be continually frustrated. Have
an open mind, but have a screen in it. God is a lot easier on
you than your husband or your wife or even yourself.

Many Christians would be indignant if you said that they
lacked faith. They say they believe in Christ, in the Bible,
and in salvation, but faith is not merely for salvation—faith
is for Christian living. The Holy Spirit can take away the
feeling of insecurity and give you a sense of being in the
center of God's love and purpose.

There are those who tell you that we can by our own will
power build up security. They warn that if we lack self-con-
fidence we shall fail, and they tell us all this without any
reference to the great spiritual universe with which we have
to deal. Psychological self-effort may bring a certain amount
of success to us, but will fail miserably when Satan with all
of his hosts attack us.

No person can of himself withstand the inevitable blows
of life, nor can he withstand the onslaughts of the Evil One.
Paul tells us we are to put on the whole armor of God that
we may be able to withstand in the evil day, that the Holy
Spirit helps us to lay hold upon the Word of God. Such passages as Romans 12:2 (A.S.V.) : "Be not fashioned according
to this world: but be ye transformed by the renewing of your

mind, that ye may prove what is the good and acceptable and perfect will of God" give us strength.

Our modern civilization—hard, clanking, brassy, disconcerting, disintegrating—destroys peace within us. It is almost impossible to avoid fuming and fretting over today's vexatious inconsistencies. Yet the Word of God says: "Fret not thyself because of evil-doers, neither be thou envious against them that work unrighteousness." Somehow or other we must find a way to turn aside as often as possible from the terrible stresses life puts upon us and find a hiding place—a place of quiet resting in the loving heart of God. Getting away from things is becoming increasingly difficult in our complex civilization. The noise and the rush and the hustle and bustle are not of God, and are deadly to peace of mind and quietness of soul. We must hear Jesus say: "My peace I leave with you, my peace I give unto you. . . . Let not your heart be troubled, neither let it be afraid."

ANTICIPATIONS

God's people must resolutely check their headlong pace or it will land them feet first in the grave. Perhaps one of the most defeating experiences is this common attitude of anticipating every difficulty that can possibly happen before we do anything. It presages defeat and sometimes so scares people that they never start anything.

If we have prayed and felt that God would have us work for Him, let us go ahead and we shall succeed, for "if God be for us, who can be against us?" The very essence of Christian success is a God-given faith. The Lord Jesus in Mark 9:23 (A.S.V.) says: "If thou canst! All things are possible to him that believeth." This is a law contrary to regular earthly procedure. In the world people say "seeing is believing"; in Christianity, "believing is seeing." "Said I not unto thee, that, if thou wouldest believe, thou shouldest see the glory of God?" When God gives us a task to do, then we can do it. It may seem impossible to us, but all things are possible with God. The athletic coach teaching the young college lad the high jump said, "Boy, if you want to get over that bar, throw your heart over it and your body will follow."

It is the old biblically-based, Holy Spirit led religion that works. It is an all-weather faith. The new "Cult of Reassurance" is conditioned to material prosperity. It is a pleasure boat, not a rugged "gospel ship." It sails well in bright seas and calm water. It is a pleasure craft and there is lots of fun on board. But watch it when the seas of trouble become mountainous waves in its path, when the howl of the tempest drowns the music of the gay voyagers. The gay bannered vessel will not be able to stand the blast. It has delightful passengers and wonderful ports of call on its itinerary, but the Captain is not on board. There is no one to still the storm of adversity and authoritatively command, "Peace, be still." Christ is not on that boat. He masters the craft of His own making. He promises no stormless voyage, but says: "I'm the Master of ocean and sea and sky. I will never leave thee nor forsake thee."

DONALD GREY BARNHOUSE

Born in Watsonville, California.

Student University of Chicago; Princeton, Princeton Theological Seminary, 1915-1917; Grenoble, France, 1923-1925; graduate student and faculty assistant, University of Pennsylvania, 1925-1927; Th.M., Eastern Baptist Theological Seminary, 1927; D.D., Dallas Theological Seminary, 1933; Th.D., Aix-en-Provence, France.

Ordained ministry Presbyterian Church, 1918; pastor, Tenth Church, Philadelphia, since 1927; Radio Preacher on CBS and NBC since 1928; editor, *Revelation*, 1931-1949, *Eternity* 1950—; member, Victorian Institute (London) ; American Scholars of Oriental Research; Chevalier of the French Legion of Honor.

Author: *God's Methods of Holy Living; Teaching the Word of Truth; Man's Ruin, God's Wrath, God's Remedy; God's River;* and others.

On Expository Preaching

EXPOSITORY PREACHING is the art of explaining the text of the Word of God, using all the experiences of life and learning to illuminate the exposition.

The prime factor in expository preaching is the belief that the Bible is the Word of God. I can speak of this only as I know it. When I take the Bible into my hands I think of it as originating with God, given by Him to man in the very order, terms, phrases, and words in which He wanted us to have it. "No prophecy ever came by the will of man, but men

29

spake from God, being moved by the Holy Spirit" (II Peter 1:21, A.S.V.).

Men who dictate letters usually instruct their secretaries to write the dictator's initials in capital letters in the lower left-hand corner of the letter, then followed by the initials of the secretary in small letters. For several years my letters bore the initials DGB/rnv. My intimate friends could identify my secretary, but they did not hold her responsible for what I wrote. In like manner I approach the Word of God as though it were signed GOD/moses or GOD/paul. My whole mentality repudiates the idea that God could have permitted His amanuenses to lessen the driving force of the divine Word. Thus, when I open the Bible to prepare a sermon, I never think of the human personality through whom the Word came, unless there is something about the writer, as occasionally there is, that will bring fresh light to the message.

I glory in all that scholarship has accomplished in lower criticism, establishing an ever more accurate text of the original languages. I give practically no consideration to anything that has been done in the field of higher criticism, although I have spent hundreds of weary hours plowing through the work of the critics, trying to find out what they are driving at, and finally rejecting their conclusions because they proceed on the false premise that the Bible originated with man and that it is the record of man's thoughts about God.

The next most important factor in expository preaching is total submission of one's entire being to the truth of the Bible as it operates in the personal life of the preacher. The man who is to thunder in the court of Pharaoh with an imperious, "Thus saith the Lord!" must first stand barefoot before the burning bush. Expressed simply and directly, God cannot use us as well when we are not fully submitted to His Word. "God is light and in him is no darkness at all. If we say we have fellowship with him and walk in darkness, we lie and do not the truth" (I John 1:5, 6).

The third factor in expository preaching is that it is a lifetime work. A man who is called to the ministry of the Word will have little time for other things. He must turn away often from many good projects. One of the great faults in the church today is that congregations take their preachers away from the Word of God to work that should be done by other men. Early in my career I preached a message on the choice of the first deacons: "And the twelve called the multitude of the disciples unto them, and said, It is not fit that we should forsake the Word of God, and serve tables. Look ye out therefore, brethren, from among you seven men of good report, full of the Spirit and of wisdom, whom we may appoint over this business. But we will continue steadfastly in prayer, and the ministry of the word" (Acts 6:2-4, A.S.V.). My deacons heeded the message and assumed their rightful task.

I have counseled many younger men in the matter of expository preaching and have advised them that it is impossible for a beginner to prepare eight or twelve good expository messages each month. I say to a young preacher, "Tell your people frankly that you are going to give studies at the midweek meeting based on the work of some great expositor. Do not be afraid to tell them that they will hear expositions by Spurgeon or Maclaren each Wednesday evening for a year. Perhaps more people will come to hear Bonar on Leviticus than would come to hear Smith or Jones on Leviticus! If you deceive them into thinking that you worked up these studies yourself, the Lord simply cannot bless your ministry. But if you let them know that you are getting your material from someone whose writing has blessed your own soul, God will bless your people through it."

My own first expository work was done in the following circumstances. When I was eighteen years old, Dr. R. A. Torrey arranged for me to hold a week of meetings in a tiny church some eighty miles from Los Angeles. I had sermons enough with me for just a week. There was great blessing, and I was invited to preach a second week; so I had to return to Los Angeles and buy several books of evangelistic sermons to see me through. I decided to speak Monday evening on John 1:12, and wrote down that verse as follows: "As many as received him, to them gave he power to become the sons of God." After writing random thoughts to be organized later, I suddenly noticed that I had left out the first word of the text. I penciled it in and, "by chance," I wrote all three letters in capitals. There it stood—"BUT." I marked it over and over until it stood out in bold face—*"BUT."* Thinking of the verbal inspiration of the Word of God, I gave attention to the meaning of that word in its context. Surely it was the hinge between preceding and following thoughts!

That evening I used the word *But* as the introduction, and before I knew it the forty-five minutes of preaching time had passed. The rest of the verse served for my study on Tuesday evening. Thus, without knowing it I had ceased to be primarily an evangelist and had become a Bible teacher. I had begun to expound the inner meaning of the Word of God.

About that time I began to memorize the Scripture. I began "by chance" with the epistle to the Philippians. In 104 days, a verse a day, I memorized the epistle, reciting it to myself at every possible opportunity. This was to prove invaluable in exposition.

While in theological seminary, I read many expositors. In Godet on *Romans* I read: "The Reformation was certainly the work of the Epistle to the Romans and that to the Galatians; and it is probable that every great spiritual renovation in the Church will always be linked, both in cause and effect, to a deeper knowledge of this book. A true knowledge of this masterpiece of the apostolic mind will always be reserved to the one who approaches with a heart 'hungering and thirsting after righteousness' as Jesus demanded in the Sermon on the Mount. For what is the Epistle to the Romans after all? It is the righteousness of God offered to the one who admits that the law has stripped him of his own righteousness. To understand such a book one must be in sympathy with the purpose that dictated it."

The reading of this paragraph set the course of my ministry. From that time on I was a preacher of the Epistle to the Romans. On my first Sunday morning as pastor of Tenth Presbyterian Church in Philadelphia, in 1927, I preached on the opening verse of the Epistle. The next Sunday I took the second verse and talked about the Gospel in the Old Testament. After three and a half years at Tenth Church, I reached the last verse in Romans, having preached from no other portion of Scripture at the Sunday morning services. During that time the congregation grew from a hundred or more to a church filled to capacity, with new life.

As a young preacher, I read perhaps half a hundred commentaries on Romans. Nowadays I confine myself to the Greek text and a score of translations and versions in several languages, using principally the Greek concordance and other master works on the vocabulary of the New Testament.

Two verses should form the framework of the expositor's thinking: "A man can receive nothing, except it be given him from heaven" (John 3:27) and: "If any man thinketh that he knoweth anything, he knoweth not yet as he ought to know" (I Cor. 8:2, A.S.V.). With this attitude, the teacher will come to a verse fresh, even though he has read it a thousand times and exegeted each word from the original on many occasions. The Word of God is always sending forth new light.

For the purpose of this volume, I have decided to present the steps in the development of a study in the Gospel of Mark, preached on a Sunday morning in the autumn of 1956.

First, I read through the Gospel of Mark in many translations and versions. When the time came to prepare the ser-

mon, I jotted down various thoughts about the particular
portion (7:24-30) that was to be studied. Then I wrote,
"Jesus and the Syro-Phenician Woman." Following that I
wrote: "He could not be hid. Callous disciples: 'Send her
away, she troubleth us.' 'Son of David!' her mistaken cry.
No reply. 'Lord!' True call brings answer. Jesus' various
answers. Persistence. Humility. The answer."

After reading and rereading the passage, I formed the
above notes into a more concrete outline, under these headings:

1. He could not be hid. 2. The woman on the road. Matthew's account. 3. The callous disciples. 4. Jesus' first answer.
5. Christ now goes into the house to rest. 6. The persistence
of the woman. 7. Phillips on Matt. 15:25. "Do please help
me, Lord!" 8. Bread for dogs? 9. Her persistence. 10. Her
humility. 11. The desired answer. 12. The unrecorded joy.

Finally, I sat down at my typewriter and wrote the following, which I took with me into the pulpit:

I. HE COULD NOT BE HID. What a truly proper and human
desire for privacy! BUT HE COULD NOT BE HID. The reason:
He had what all men need. Thus He fulfilled His own statement about the ministry: "Whosoever would become great
among you shall be your minister; and whosoever would be
first among you shall be your servant" (Matt. 20:26, A.S.V.).
HE COULD NOT BE HID because, being the greatest, He was the
bondslave of all. It was love that drove Him to this.

II. THE WOMAN ON THE ROAD. Matthew tells the story to
show that the whole incident took place in two parts: one
on the road in the morning, the other in the house after mid-
day. Mark describes only the final scene. But she had first
come to Him on the road. "Son of David, Son of David!"
(Matt. 15:21 ff.). This shows her ignorance and her faith.
She had heard about Him from someone who gave her information about Him, using His Jewish name. Thus she

approached Him with a Jewish title. Naturally, He could do nothing for her then.

III. CALLOUSNESS OF THE DISCIPLES. This hardness resulted from failure to look through Christ's eyes; a failure to be fully possessed by Him. Selfishness. No compassion. "Send her away, she crieth after us!" What a commentary on the selfishness of the clergy!

IV. JESUS' FIRST ANSWER: "I am not sent but unto the lost sheep of the house of Israel."

V. NOW, MARK'S ACCOUNT. JESUS IN THE HOUSE. He could not be hid. Need of rest, but interrupted by need.

VI. THE PERSISTENCE OF THE WOMAN. Why was she so persistent? Only one answer. SHE LOVED HER DAUGHTER. It is as simple as that. She prayed for her daughter who was not able to pray for herself. She did not stop until she received her answer. By coming to Christ she got that which she had not been able to get from any human means. THE GIRL DIDN'T SAY A WORD. THE MOTHER SPOKE FOR HER AND GOT THE ANSWER. MANY INSTANCES OF THIS (nobleman for his son; centurion for his servant; Jairus for his daughter). James 5:16: "The effectual fervent prayer of a righteous man availeth much."

VII. Phillips translates Matthew 15:25: "Do please help me, Lord!" Different word on her lips. No longer "Son of David," but "Lord."

VIII. CHILDREN'S BREAD . . . DOGS. Did Christ call a woman a dog? Yes, He did. But note: Two Greek words for dogs. *Kuon*, primitive word; we would say curs. *Kuon* licked Lazarus' sores. Give not that which is holy to *kuon* (Matt. 7:6). Beware of *kuon* (Phil. 3:2). The *kuon* is returned to his own vomit (II Peter 2:22). Without are *kuon* (Rev. 22:15). But here is another word, *kunarion*—used only in this story. Lexicon says, "puppy." He had to judge the woman and show her her Gentile position; but *He used the nicest word available* that was consistent with the truth.

IX. HER PERSISTENCE. Pray for your children. I have known of cases where grown men and women would not allow their parents to speak to them about the Lord. But *no child can prevent the parent from speaking to the Lord about him.*

X. HER HUMILITY. "All right, Lord. Give me the crumbs of grace. Crumbs for dogs!"

XI. THE DESIRED ANSWER. Phillips: "You can go home." "And her daughter was healed from that hour" (A.S.V.).

XII. THERE IS NO DESCRIPTION OF HER JOY. The Holy Spirit knows you can understand that.

The above is what I took into the pulpit, and the words flowed over the top of the pulpit like molten silver. The tape recording that day registered every dangling participial clause, every sloppy sentence, every departure from a finished sentence occasioned by the rise of new, warm thoughts which came crowding to be preached. The result was that although the exposition was not smoothly literary or rhetorical, it was alive. Expository preaching must be direct and simple, if the hearer is to assimilate it.

The next chapter in this book is a sermon on another theme. The manner of preparation was much like that described above, but it has been polished until it has assumed the form of a coin, rather than molten metal. I am honest enough, I hope, to recognize a difference in coins. I have called it silver, not gold. I know that it is not like the modern coin of great hardness, stamped out by the hydraulic press. Ancient coins were poured into molds from liquid metal. They were soft, and their edges could be sliced away. If this were done often enough, the coin became lightweight—*adokimos,* the word Paul uses in I Corinthians 9:27 for "castaway," or "disqualified." The Lord knows I have tried never to cut the edges of my coins. But, like Paul, I still tremble.

Living from the Word of God

DONALD GREY BARNHOUSE

IN EPHESIANS 6:17, 18 we read: "Take the helmet of salvation, and the sword of the Spirit, which is the word of God; praying always with all prayer and supplication in the Spirit, and watching thereunto with all perseverance and supplication for all saints."

Now notice that the Holy Spirit is mentioned twice: "Take . . . the sword of the Spirit," and pray at all times in the Spirit. He is mentioned in connection with the Bible and with prayer. These two means are given to us by God to overcome the enemy and live in triumph. Although the Word of God and prayer are to be used as offensive and defensive weapons, here the Bible is presented as our weapon for offense—the sword of the Spirit against the enemy, while prayer is to be used both offensively and defensively.

How is the Bible our weapon of offense? The Greek word here translated "Word of God" is not *logos,* which denotes the divine revelation from Genesis to the end of the Bible. It is *rhema;* it means a word as part of a sentence, a sentence as part of a discourse, a portion of the whole. In spiritual conflict, one cannot use the whole Bible in one encounter, but a single passage is sufficient to defeat Satan.

This was demonstrated by the Lord Jesus Christ when He used three verses from the Book of Deuteronomy to resist Satan in the wilderness. Jesus answered: "It is written, Man shall not live by bread alone, but by every word that pro-

37

ceeds out of the mouth of God. . . . It is written, thou shalt
not tempt the Lord thy God. . . . It is written, thou shalt worship the Lord thy God and him only shalt thou serve" (Deut.
8:3; 6:16, 13). The Lord Jesus had such a grasp of the Bible
that He could use a passage from any part to meet the at-
tacks of the tempter. When He was twelve years old, He con-
founded the doctors in the Temple and showed a knowledge
of the Scriptures beyond that of the religious leaders of Israel.

At the beginning of our Lord's ministry, as we read in
Luke 4: He came to Nazareth where he had been brought
up; and he went into the synagogue, as his custom was, on
the sabbath day. And he stood up to read and there was
given to him the book of the prophet Isaiah. He opened the
book and found the place. Note the phrase, He "found
the place." Many Christians read the Bible so little that they
have difficulty finding the place when the preacher indicates
the text of his message, or the passage to be read responsively.
I have heard a Christian ask, "Is Romans in the Old Testament or the New?" And again, "Where in the Old Testament is the Book of Hebrews?" To become familiar with the
Bible and its structure, you must spend time reading it and
looking up passages. How can you experience the power,
victory, and peace necessary to Christian triumph if you do
not possess the Word of God in your heart and mind?

Psalm 1 describes the blessedness of "the man who walketh
not in the counsel of the ungodly, nor standeth in the way
of sinners, nor sitteth in the seat of the scornful. But his
DELIGHT is in the law of the Lord; and in his law doth he
meditate day and night." Now, this last clause does not mean
that life is to be spent entirely in meditation, with no time
to earn daily bread and pursue regular duties. "Meditate
day and night" is a Hebraism which indicates that all life
and living are to be within the sphere of the Bible. The Christian is bound by the Word of God, but it does not hamper

him. Rather, it enlarges his vision and enables him to see far beyond anything that the unsaved man can see.

Suppose you walk to a hilltop on a clear night and find several men there, gazing at the stars. You ask, "What are you doing?" They reply, "We are making a star map and are counting the stars." And you say, "Follow me, and I shall show you more stars than you can imagine. Come into this observatory and put your eye to the lens of a telescope." "What!" they exclaim. "You want us to leave this vast sweep of the heavens and peer through a one-inch piece of glass?" Exactly so. If they will cease to view the heavens with the naked eye and confine themselves to the lens of a telescope, they will learn more than they ever knew before about the stars. If you, in the spiritual realm will leave the little hilltop of your natural point of view and submit to the Word of God, you will receive supernatural vision and see all that God has set before you. Psalm 119:104 says: "Through thy precepts I get understanding; therefore I hate every false way."

The Bible must come first in the Christian's life, if he is to know power and peace. The Chinese preacher Leland Wang followed the rule, "No Bible, no breakfast." "For," said he, "if I do not have breakfast I can live on my fat till noon, but if I go without the Word of God I am always faint before noon." How many Christians in the West need to learn that lesson!

An anonymous English preacher has written, "As life goes on there comes to most of us a clearer view of its meaning and of its lessening importance. The words 'This is not your rest' gain fresh meaning as the years go by. And another truth is borne in upon us; namely, that we are surrounded by strange hidden forces, harassed by unseen foes and that the more deliberately we try to live with a high aim in view the more surely we are battered and assaulted. The more we realize that even now we are fellow citizens of the saints and of the household of God, the more we find war and strife to be our portion."

In other words, the closer you wish to come to God, the more Satan will tempt you to fall short in giving time to the Bible, and even to abandon reading it. We must find our victory in the Word of God, and we must give ourselves to it, for that reason.

Instead of mounting up with wings as eagles, many, many Christians grovel in the dust of defeat. Why? Is it not because they live in alternating cycles of committing sin and then being sorry and confessing it to God? How many Christians get out of the will of God, then weep and vow that it shall not happen again, only to be defeated a short time later! Why is this so? Has not God given the power to live our daily lives in victory? Are we unable to obey Him? If you are born again, God has given you power to triumph and to do His will. Beyond question, He has made it possible for us to overcome through Christ who strengthens us. He has planted new life within us. He has made us partakers of His divine nature. What, then, do we lack? We lack plain, simple determination to do what God wants us to do, and to use what He has given us to use. So the Holy Spirit tells us in Ephesians 6:10: "Be strong in the Lord, and in the power of his might."

When a child of God uses the Bible in simple dependence upon Him, Satan is powerless. James 4:7 says: "Submit yourselves therefore to God. Resist the devil and he will flee from you." You will never triumph until you definitely and determinedly use the Word of God as the sword of the Spirit. Satan knows this; he will go to any lengths to turn your attention from the Bible. He will use every means to cause you to relax your hold upon the sword, or to dull its blade. What can loosen your hold upon the sword of the Spirit? Nothing but sin.

Some years ago, a college girl came to me for counsel; in

her face I saw sorrow and gloom as she said, "I was a strong Christian in my home town, but since I came to college I have gotten away from the Lord. I am not even interested in church any more." I asked, "Are you sure that you are trusting in Christ as your personal Saviour?" "Oh, yes!" she said. Then I asked, "What are your Bible-reading habits?" She replied, "I used to read the Bible every day, but I have not read it for several months." (Our conversation took place in the spring of the year.) Then I asked her, "Can you recall the approximate date on which you last read the Bible?" She said, "About November 20, just before Thanksgiving." Looking her straight in the eye I said, "What happened about November 15?" She burst out crying and told me that then she had gotten out of the will of God and committed sin. Within five days she could no longer tolerate the Word of God. After a prayer of confession, she was restored to fellowship, and her life became strong in the Lord and in the power of His might, as once again she took up the sword of the Spirit.

As we read the Psalms, we discovered that David knew the importance of wielding this sword of the Spirit. There were several incidents in his life of which he was later ashamed. Like the college girl, he too repented and poured out his heart to God: "Have mercy upon me, O God, according to thy lovingkindness; according to the multitude of thy tender mercies, blot out my transgressions. Wash me throughly from mine iniquity and cleanse me from my sin. For I acknowledge my transgressions: and my sin is ever before me. Against thee, thee only, have I sinned, and done this evil in thy sight: that thou mightest be justified when thou speakest, and be clear when thou judgest. . . . Create in me a clean heart, O God; and renew a right spirit within me. . . . Restore unto me the joy of thy salvation; and uphold me with thy free spirit" (Ps. 51:1-4, 10, 12). But David did not stop with mere repentance. He knew the value of wielding the sword of the Spirit. In another psalm we read: "Wherewithal shall a young man cleanse his way? by taking heed thereto according to thy word. With my whole heart have I sought thee: O let me not wander from thy commandments. Thy word have I hid in mine heart, that I might not sin against thee. Blessed art thou, O Lord: teach me thy statutes" (Ps. 119:9-12).

Now, what will dull the edge of the sword? Doubt in the mind of the Christian. To overcome doubts, we must live in the sphere of the Book. Everything we do or think must be cast into the mold of the Bible. If our lives are not conformed to it, there can be no triumph.

All that I have been saying comes close to the heart of the Gospel, which Paul defines in I Corinthians 15:1, 3, 4: "This is the gospel which I have preached unto you [1] that Christ died for our sins according to the scriptures; [2] that he was buried; [3] that he rose again the third day according to the scriptures." Let us analyze this. Once Paul says that Christ died for our sins. Once he says that He was buried. Once Paul says that He rose again. Twice it is stated that all was *according to the Scriptures.*

Now let us turn to Ephesians 6:18 and see the place of prayer in the life of the believer. God so orders life that we must constantly turn to Him. No detail is too small for His love and interest. In I Thessalonians 5:18 God says: "In everything give thanks; for this is the will of God in Christ Jesus concerning you"—that you should pray about everything. When we get up in the morning we should say, "Lord, I want to honor You today in what I wear, in what I eat, in all that I do." Of course the first act of the day is to read the Bible and talk with God. The outcome of the day hangs on this. At your work, where people have coffee breaks, you may have prayer breaks. You finish a column of figures and straighten up for a moment to get the kinks out of your back. You can say, "Lord, I love You and need You. Help me to do my job well." This is the will of God, that we by good works silence the mouths of evildoers. Instead of saying, "Oh, he is just a religious fanatic," your employer should be saying, "Nobody here turns out as much work as he does!"

Some years ago I was driving south through Tampa, Florida, when suddenly I got a flat tire. In the morning I had read this verse, "In everything give thanks," and had determined to thank God for anything that might happen during that day. I now leaned over the steering wheel and said, "Lord, I thank Thee for this flat tire." It seemed slightly absurd to thank God for such a thing, but I thanked Him that all the events of life are in His hands, even a flat tire. I telephoned for a repair truck, and while waiting I emptied the trunk of a load of books so that we could get the spare tire out. When the repair man saw the books, he picked one up and said, "Religion! Are you a preacher?" I replied, "Yes, I am. Do you know the Lord Jesus Christ as your Saviour?" He said, "Well, I don't believe I am saved." While he changed the tire, I told him of the love of Christ and of his need to receive Him as Saviour and Lord. Right there he said, "I will stop trusting in myself and commit myself to Christ and put my trust in Him." Several years passed, and the incident faded from my mind. But when I was preaching in another city in Florida, after the service a man came to me and reminded me of the flat tire in Tampa. I asked him what he was doing, and he replied, "Since I took the Lord as my Saviour I have moved to this town and am now a deacon in the Baptist church." You see, God had a purpose in allowing that tire to go flat. The ways of God, so mysterious to us, are all known to Him. He knows the way that we take; we can trust Him and give thanks "in everything."

Finally, I want you to note the relationship between prayer and the Bible, between the sword of the Spirit and praying in the Spirit. Blessed indeed are those who keep in constant touch with the Lord, turning to Him in every situation and seeking His guidance in every choice. Our text tells us to pray always with all prayer and supplication. In prayer we are occupied with God Himself. In supplication we are occupied with our needs and those of others. In prayer we think about Him: about His glories, His work, and His worship. In supplication we petition God for ourselves, for our own needs, and for those of others.

In the chapter and verse structure of the Bible it is unfortunate that verses 17 and 18 of Ephesians 6 are divided, for they form one sentence: "Take the sword of the Spirit which is the word of God, praying at all times." Does this not show us that God considers Bible reading inseparable from prayer? And prayer inseparable from the Bible? God has given us His Word to show us our nothingness and to reveal the Lord Jesus Christ; to teach us that all our need is met in Him, to bring us into oneness with our Lord, and to conform us to His image. Those who use the Bible apart from prayer degenerate into philosophical theologians. Those who pray without sound Bible knowledge lapse into sickly sentimentality and emotionalism which are alien to the vigorous life of the Holy Spirit.

The man who reads the Bible without being filled with the Spirit in prayer will become cold, pedantic, intellectual. God has given us the Word and prayer, joined together by the indwelling Holy Spirit. When we study the Bible prayerfully, we increase in the knowledge of God and His ways; when we pray in the Spirit in the light of the Word, our devotion is spiritual instead of psychological; all will center in Jesus Christ.

For this God works in us, through His Word and prayer, that we might center our lives in Christ and become more like Him day by day.

HOWARD W. FERRIN

Born in Auburn, New York.

Moody Bible Institute; University of Chicago; A.B., North-western, 1922; LL.D., Houghton College, New York, 1947.

Pastor, White City Gospel Tabernacle, 1922-1925; president, Providence-Barrington Bible College, 1925—; president, Africa Inland Mission, 1947-56. Conference speaker and traveler and radio preacher.

Author: *I Believe; Unto All; Studies in Romans; Living Above; Twelve Portraits; The Riddle of the Middle East.*

A Distinctive Style

IT IS SAID that every baseball player has his distinctive style. This is especially true of batters. Good catchers study the distinguishing pecularities of each batter in order to signal the pitcher what mystifying pitches should be delivered. What is true of baseball players is also true of preachers. Each preacher has his own distinctive personal traits. Nowhere is this more evident than in the character and quality of sermons which he delivers.

Some years ago there were two brothers, one of whom was a baseball pitcher and the other a preacher. The salary of the pitcher was $15,000 whereas the salary of the preacher was $1500. In conversation one day the preacher lamented the difference in salaries and asked the question: "Why is it that for delivering a ball across the plate you get $15,000 while I get only $1500 for delivering a sermon?" The broth-

er replied: "Well, brother, I guess it is all in the *delivery!*"
Much truth is often spoken in jest. The delivery of a sermon
is important, for whatever the character and content of the
sermon, much of its success—at least much of its immediate
success—depends upon the manner in which it is presented.
Sometimes good delivery will make a poor sermon effective,
whereas the effects of a good sermon can be nullified by
poor and shoddy delivery. A preacher should seek in every
way to improve his delivery lest his good sermons fail to produce the desired results. This can only be done by diligent
preparation.

In my thirty-five years of ministry, I have served as a pastor no more than ten years. My experience in preparing
sermons, therefore, has differed from that of those preachers
whose responsibilities require them to produce sermons
weekly. Those ten years, however, provided an early discipline in sermon building. Two of the churches I served
were new churches and called for sermons of an evangelistic
and expository character. My evangelistic sermons were
mainly textual in character, with an occasional sermon based
upon some Biblical story or incident. As a young preacher,
I found the demand for two sermons weekly a formidable
one. I feverishly went about collecting materials from every
available source. The most effective way I found of doing
this was by the use of *Wilson's Topical and Textual Index.*
The investment of twenty dollars in this index some thirty
years ago has paid off a hundredfold. While in later years
I have not had recourse to it as much as in the early days
of my ministry, it still is a reservoir from which I may repeatedly draw needed material. It may have its weaknesses,
but I have not found them. My sermons were largely con-
structed on the traditional three-point structure, and Spurgeon was my teacher. What a poor pupil he has had!

In more recent years the pattern of my sermon building
has altered, due to several causes. First, my association with

Providence-Barrington Bible College provided me with the unexcelled privilege of classroom teaching, particularly in the fields of the Pauline Epistles, and both Biblical and Systematic Theology. Obviously my mind was conditioned by such studies. My sermons, therefore, began to take on a more theological flavor, which was evident also in my radio preaching. For example, for the radio audience I prepared a series of twenty sermons on the Apostles' Creed. I also gave a series of studies on I Peter. It was gratifying to know there were listeners who wanted sermons of an expository character with a strong Biblical and doctrinal emphasis and expressed that desire by requesting that these sermons be published.

The second cause of alteration in my sermons was due to a greater respect for the sermon itself. In my youth I thought that the louder I spoke and the faster I talked, the better the sermon! The exciting freedom that I enjoyed in those days was exhilarating indeed, but I am quite sure now that my congregation did not appreciate it as much as I did! The content of my sermons suffered often at the expense of ad-libbing which must have been at times insufferably thin! As I matured, I began to have more respect for my congregations and a higher esteem of a good sermon. I began to read and, as opportunity was granted, to hear well-prepared sermons delivered effectively by able preachers. This, I have discovered, is one of the best preparations one can have in improving the quality of one's sermons. In more recent years I have sought to give more careful preparation to my sermons while, at the same time not forfeiting, I trust, the fervor that I knew in my youth. Careful preparation was really forced upon me because I have been required, for many years, to prepare radio scripts. This is one of the finest of disciplines for the preacher. If one has only ten or fifteen minutes to speak, he studies more diligently how he can strengthen each sentence and eliminate that which is not pertinently relevant to the subject. I am sure that no virile sermon has ever been produced that has not been the subject of review and rewriting not only once, but several times. The skill to produce better sermons is a cultivated one.

As I have attempted to analyze how I prepare my sermons, I have concluded that in more recent years they have not been the result of any systematic or formal preparation in my study, but are largely the result of my confrontation with life and its challenges.

A distinguished minister of the Church of Scotland once said that his sermons fell into two classes: those that came to him as on the wings of a bird, and those that were a long time in the making—the fruit of long hours of strenuous work. I think that more of mine come "as on the wings of a bird" than otherwise. Let me illustrate: I was invited to preach to several hundred people who were taking a boat trip in October on Lake Winnipesaukee to see the glory of the autumnal colors of our magnificent New England hills and valleys. No sermon on hand seemed fitting. What text or theme would be appropriate? While traveling along the highway a few days before the boat trip I was overwhelmed with the breath-taking splendor of the fall. Then I thought: "How good is our God to give us such glory as this to see, and eyes with which to see it." Then there flashed into my mind Romans 2:4. I had never preached nor heard a sermon on it: "The goodness of God leadeth thee to repentance." The outline came immediately: The glory of God's creation; the goodness of His providence and the grace of His redemption. These three manifestations of God's goodness should most surely lead men to repentance. While traveling the next day, the sermon took on "flesh" and seemed quite full and complete upon delivery.

One of the most decisive elements in producing better sermons is that the preacher himself becomes a better Christian. Only when his own life is enriched can he enrich the lives of others. "Like preacher, like people." A preacher must ever reach out after the larger dimensions of life which make for full and effective living. There must be a breadth, depth, and height to his experience if these dimensions are to be found in his sermons. There must be a mature understanding of the interrelationships of life with their many involvements, if one is to help people understand themselves, suggest solutions to their many and varied problems and strengthen them in the faith. The preacher must himself grapple with and resolve his own doubts in order better to sympathize with and understand the doubts of others. He must lay well the foundation of his own faith, if he is to lay the cornerstone upon which others must build. He must himself draw heavily upon God's grace if he is to encourage his people to avail themselves of God's all-sufficient provision in Christ for joyous daily living. He must himself be inspired by hope and courage if he is to provide that inspiration for others and, above all things, he must himself live in the light of eternity if he is to cast any light upon the pilgrim pathway of those who journey through this world's night to the celestial day.

The preacher must be the best sermon his people ever see or hear. This can only be as he assiduously cultivates his own spiritual life. Some years ago I read the secret of George Mueller's spiritual life in his autobiography. It has been sort of a model to me ever since. It suggests to every Christian, and I think especially to the preacher, the way by which one can prepare himself better than in any other way for not only sermon-making, but for the fulfillment of every responsibility of life and ministry. This is a somewhat lengthy quotation, but the contents thereof are so absolutely vital to the maintenance of the Christian life of the servant of Christ that I venture to give it:

> It pleased the Lord to teach me a truth . . . the benefit
> of which I have not lost . . . more than forty years. The

point is this: I saw more clearly than ever, that the first great and primary business to which I ought to attend every day was to have my soul happy in the Lord. The first thing to be concerned about was not, how much I might serve the Lord, how much I might glorify the Lord; but how I might get my soul into a happy state, and how my inner man might be nourished. For I might seek to set the truth before the unconverted, I might seek to benefit believers, I might seek to relieve the distressed, I might in other ways seek to behave myself as it becomes a child of God in this world; and yet, not being happy in the Lord, and not being nourished and strengthened in my inner man day by day, all this might not be attended to in a right spirit. Before this time my practice had been, at least for ten years previously, as an habitual thing, to give myself to prayer, after having dressed myself in the morning. Now, I saw that the most important thing I had to do was to give myself to the reading of the Word of God, and to meditation on it that thus my heart might be comforted, encouraged, warned, reproved, instructed, and that thus . . . whilst meditating, my heart might be brought into experimental communion with the Lord.

I began, therefore, to meditate on the New Testament, from the beginning, early in the morning. The first thing I did, after having asked in a few words the Lord's blessing upon His precious Word, was to begin to meditate on the Word of God, searching, as it were, into every verse, to get blessing out of it; not for the sake of the public ministry of the Word; not for the sake of preaching on what I had meditated upon; but for the sake of obtaining food for my own soul. The result I have found to be almost invariably this, that after a very few minutes my soul has been led to confession . . . or to supplication; so that though I did not, as it were, give myself to prayer, but to meditation, yet it turned almost immediately more or less into prayer.[1]

[1]G. Fred Bergin (comp.), *Autobiography of George Mueller*, London: Pickering & Inglis, 1929.

Some sermons, however, have been long in the making. Such is the sermon I have submitted to be included in this volume: "What Price Education?" Since I have been engaged in the educational field for more than thirty years, I have tried to keep abreast of the part education has played in contemporary life and thought. In the sermon I refer to the fact that while there have been those who have put their hope in education as being the savior of mankind, I was skeptical of any education that was not distinctly Christian in character. I have labored this point on the basis that no society is orderly unless its system of culture and social relationships is well integrated. If there is confusion, social unrest, and an excessive spirit of conflict in the body politic, it is evidently due to the fact that there is something basically wrong at the center of man's thinking. Therefore it is important to inquire as to what has been the core of modern thought during the past few centuries. That is, what has been the focal point or the unifying principle of man's life, thought, and action? My conviction is that it has been *man* himself, rather than God. With that full confidence in himself, modern man has believed that he was quite able to save himself since he was inherently good and evolving to even higher levels of life. He needed no help from God.

No longer is this view of man held seriously by our most profound thinkers. Contemporary thought as expressed in the philosophical and theological fields by such writers as Kierkegaard, Dostoevski, Barth, Tillich, Sorokin, and Niebuhr has negatived this concept. While none of these profound students of human affairs are evangelical in the strict theological sense, their thinking has strengthened the general position that man is a sinner and stands in need of the redemption which God has provided in Christ Jesus. Since the average man, consciously or unconsciously, imbibes the overtones of the thinking of our most profound students, preachers should be sensitive to the atmosphere in which the contemporary thinking of even the "man of the street" is being done.

The task of the preacher in this new age is a challenging one. There is a universalizing process going on in every area of life. All the modern means of communication and transportation are aids to condition people on all continents to think more alike than ever before. To relate Christian truth to this growing universal mind has been a task which I have attempted to do, though I feel with only minor success.

This attempt has determined quite generally the character of my sermons, within the past fifteen years in particular. To put it another way: my sermons have more or less grown out of my conscious and subconscious thinking concerning the relevancy of the Christian revelation to modern man in his present dilemma. Materials for such sermons are gathered from the contemporary literature and isolated articles which come under my observation. Extracts from serious works are often lifted to be incorporated into the structure of the sermon in order to enforce the Biblical truth being presented. Such sermons are long in the making, but I am fully convinced that they will prove to be the most helpful and stimulating to troubled minds and distressed spirits today because they point up the all-sufficiency of Christ; the relevancy of the Bible to modern life, thought, and action; and the quickening power of the Holy Spirit by which alone the intellectual, moral, and spiritual needs of modern man can be adequately met.

The True Teachers

HOWARD W. FERRIN

SHORTLY BEFORE HIS DEATH, the great English novelist, H. G. Wells, said: "The salvation of western civilization depends upon the outcome of a race between education and catastrophe." What a startling statement, yet no thoughtful person will dispute it. A tragic alternative: on the one hand —education; on the other—catastrophe.

If then the salvation of western civilization depends on the outcome of a race between education and catastrophe, it would seem quite fitting that we should ask what is to be the kind of education by which we hope to be saved. In the light of this question, it is not encouraging to listen to some of our leading educators. For instance, in the Storrs Lectures, delivered at Yale University by former Chancellor Robert Maynard Hutchins of the University of Chicago, and which have since been published under the title *Higher Learning in America,* Dr. Hutchins boldly asserts that "higher education in this country is in a state of general cultural chaos." So we face dilemma—civilization is to be saved from catastrophe by an education filled with chaos! If this be the only prospect before us, we are indeed in a dangerous condition.

It is not unthinkable that total collapse will overtake our generation. In fact, our knowledge of history—and especially of the prophetic Word—leads us to believe as Goethe puts it, "Man's history will end in man's judgment." But since we do not know when the final judgment will overtake us, it might be possible to block the juggernaut of catastrophe for a season by turning back to a true educational principle found at the heart of Christian experience.

Before we consider what this principle is, let us raise the question as to why modern man stands on the brink of a possible world collapse. One of the basic observations which must ever be kept in mind in seeking to appraise the world situation is that a society is orderly only when its system of culture and social relationships is well integrated. If there is confusion, social unrest, and an excessive spirit of conflict in the body politic, it is evidently due to the fact that there is something wrong in the center of man's thinking. Therefore it is important to inquire as to what has been the core of modern thought during the past few centuries; that is, what has been the focal point or the unifying principle of man's life, thought, and action.

It would seem to me that the dominant note in man's thinking during the past few centuries has been *man himself*. This was not true during medieval days. In that period the dominant note was *God*. The total life of western Europe was theocentric. At the beginning of the Renaissance, and more particularly since the enlightenment period at the end of the eighteenth century, man turned his thoughts upon *himself*. Where man had formerly talked about the kingdom of God, now he was talking about the kingdom of *man*. During the enlightenment period the emphasis was upon "liberty, equality, and fraternity." Man considered first his own rights. Often, if not quite generally, he disregarded the rights of God over man. He began to enjoy a degree of so-called freedom which he had not experienced in other days. As the most flourishing expression of this spirit in modern times we have Communism. The idealistic claim of Communism is that it will bring about the emancipation of man. In that sense it is a religion, and as a religion it has its eschatology. It is to bring in the kingdom of man on earth. The Messianic hope lies in the proletariat. Marx believed that the proletariat is to be the revolutionary savior of mankind and the harbinger of a true, classless community. Man is conceived of as the ultimate in life and in history. Everything is on a horizontal plane. Salvation lies in the betterment of man's economic welfare. This is the banner around which he rallies. This is the fire that burns within his breast. Let no one say that the communist passion for social righteousness is altogether evil. It has some elements in it that call for our admiration. True, there are weaknesses in its basic assumptions, but there is just enough of the good in it to make men believe that it is the ultimate for which they must strive. As the quintessence of Humanism, it makes a strong appeal to modern man.

But what is the basic weakness of Communism? What is its fatal lie? The fatal lie is that *man is his own god.* The very essence of Communism lies in its teaching of the "man-God," whereas Christianity sets forth the glorious teaching of the "God-man." The communist believes he can save himself and society. He needs no help from above.

It was during the eighteenth and nineteenth centuries that Humanism reached its height. Man was conceived of as inherently good and therefore had no need of a Saviour. No longer was he to be thought of as a partaker of Adam's original sin and born into iniquity. New psychological concepts of man were advanced which affirmed his Godlike qualities. If man would rise up and shake off the shackles of imperialism, capitalism, and conservatism, he would bring about a Utopia of prosperity and peace unparalleled in history.

Marx and Lenin were honestly convinced that when once the "classless society" had been established, the state would "wither away." Nothing could be more contrary to what has happened. Universal suffrage has brought about stateism, and the nonpossessing majority has instructed the state to auction off the worldly goods of the unrepresented minority in order to make a classless society. We have the revolt of the masses, and the *mass man*. He wants everything brought down to his own level. He is not interested in Heaven. He is interested only in this earth. He is not interested in the kingdom of God; he is only interested in the kingdom of man. This blinding optimism prevailed throughout the nineteenth century.

One of the great tragedies of our time is that liberal theologians became a prey to this lying philosophy of man's inherent goodness. The Reformation was a mighty movement. It established again the truth that man is a sinner, that he is lost and undone and cannot save himself. Man needs a Saviour and needs to be regenerated if he is to become an heir of God. But then a Neo-Protestant movement set in at just about the same time as the enlightenment period swept the earth. Theology was radically altered. It was no longer God-centered. It became man-centered. The philosophy of man's natural goodness dominated its theological concepts. The idea that man is sinful at the very center of his personality—that is, in his will—was universally rejected. The Christian doctrine of sin was almost driven from the field by the doctrine of determinism. Man was a machine and could do only what his physical constitution determined he should do. It was this new view of man that seemed to make the Christian Gospel simply irrelevant to modern man.

Then came a world crisis! Man's scientific and technological achievements turned out to be a Frankenstein monster. It is no wonder that today he fears himself more than anything else. He begins to realize that his basic problems are moral and theological rather than material. He fears that unless some light breaks through into our contemporary darkness, he is going to blow himself to bits, hence a great deal of talk today about recovery of morality in our time. In fact, men will talk about religion and plead for the "spiritual," but to me it is a serious question as to whether they are thinking deeply enough, even about themselves. Unless they realize that man is not essentially good, that he is diseased at the root of his being, that even his best intentions are frustrated by an inherent defect and that he is utterly lost in the sight of God, modern man will still be deceiving himself.

There are some of our modern thinkers who see that the doctrine of man's natural goodness has already been shattered by man's conduct in the twentieth century. One of the most astute students of human affairs is Pitirim A. Sorokin, Chairman of the Sociology Department of Harvard, who writes: "The more we study man, his conduct and psychology, the stronger grows the conviction that he in nowise resembles the 'good little boy' that the eighteenth century and the modern rationalisms love to depict. . . . Before us we have not only a sensible being, but the elemental man, who is not only peace-loving, altruistic, compassionate, but also full of rancor, cruelty, bestiality; not only consciously clear-sighted, but often blind; not only gentle and creative, but wild and destructive. . . . The quantity and quality of man's impulses and reflexes rend him, singularly, like a bomb full of different kinds of forces and tendencies capable of bursting and presenting us with a picture of wild disorder." To use Pascal's words: "Man is like an angel with a devil hidden beneath."

It is at this point that Christianity comes with its age-old teaching concerning man and his nature.

Let us now read the Scripture portion for this message:

> Now when he was in Jerusalem at the passover, in the feast day, many believed in his name, when they saw the· miracles which he did. But Jesus did not commit himself unto them, because he knew all men, and needed not that any should testify of man: for he knew what was in man.
>
> There was a man of the Pharisees, named Nicodemus, a ruler of the Jews: The same came to Jesus by night,

and said unto him, Rabbi, we know that thou art a
teacher come from God: for no man can do these miracles that thou doest, except God be with him.

Jesus answered and said unto him, Verily, verily, I say
unto thee, Except a man be born again, he cannot see
the kingdom of God. Nicodemus saith unto him, How
can a man be born when he is old? can he enter the second time into his mother's womb, and be born?

Jesus answered, Verily, verily, I say unto thee, Except
a man be born of water and of the Spirit, he cannot enter into the kingdom of God. That which is born of the
flesh is flesh; and that which is born of the Spirit is spirit.

Marvel not that I said unto thee, Ye must be born
again. The wind bloweth where it listeth, and thou
hearest the sound thereof, but canst not tell whence it
cometh, and whither it goeth: so is every one that is born
of the Spirit (John 2:23—3:8).

In His conversation with Nicodemus, Christ, the greatest
of teachers, gave us the most profound revelation concerning
man. Observe the connection of the last verses of John 2 with
John 3. Notice that He was suspicious of men. We read in
John 2:24, 25: "But Jesus did not commit himself unto
them, because he knew all men, and needed not that any
should testify of man: for he knew what was in man." This
does not mean that He did not love man, nor that He did
not see in man something which was redeemable. But since
He knew what was in man, that is, in his unregenerate state,
He would not trust him. His confidence could not be put in
fallen man. On the one hand He recognized that man in
his natural state could go a long way on his own. Indeed,
he might so cultivate himself that he would be somewhat
exemplary from a moral and religious standpoint. Nicodemus was proof of this view. He was a teacher in Israel,
and evidently a very religious man. On the other hand, our
Lord recognized that there was something fundamentally

wrong at the very bottom of man's nature, for He knew all men.

Observe the essence of His teaching in this Scripture portion. He dismissed the flattering words of Nicodemus at once and gave the conversation an entirely new direction. He wasted no time; He minced no words. He made him overhaul his entire thinking concerning himself and his own nature. He said: "Nicodemus, except a man be born from above, he cannot see the kingdom of God. So let's deal with basic things. Let's talk about *you.* You are a man born of the flesh, and that which is born of the flesh is flesh. It may be moral, it may even be religious, but it is not spiritual. It is not of God. It is not born of God. It cannot see the kingdom of God. Surely it cannot enter that kingdom. You may build your own kingdom on this earth. You may have moral and religious elements in that kingdom which make you feel that that is all you need. But it is still of yourself; it is still of the flesh. It is not of the Spirit.

"Do you not see, Nicodemus, that if you want to build on yourself, you do not trust God at all; whereas if you trust God, you discount yourself? You must put your confidence either in yourself and in your ability to build your own kingdom, or you must put your confidence in God and in His ability. God is seeking to build a kingdom that cannot be moved; a kingdom consisting of men who have been born of His Spirit and who shall ultimately be conformed to the image of His Son. So, Nicodemus, except you be born again, you cannot see, you cannot enter the kingdom of God."

Nicodemus called our Lord a "teacher." And so He was, and perhaps in no other instance did He show Himself an abler and truer teacher than at this time, for a true teacher is one who must think rightly about both God and man. If he has a false notion of either God or man, he cannot be a true teacher of mankind. There are many profound lessons that he must teach, but we are convinced that the truth of the new birth is a basic fundamental. While he cannot stop at this level, he must build his superstructure on that foundation or else it will ultimately totter and fall, and that for several reasons.

First: If a teacher does not know this truth, if he does not believe it, if he himself has not been born of God, he cannot qualify as a true Christian teacher. Only as he is born again, only as he has come to see himself as insufficient, sinful, and in need of a Saviour, and only as he sees in Jesus Christ that Saviour will his eyes be opened to see things spiritual. If he has not been born again, the Lord might well say to him what He said to Nicodemus: "Art thou a teacher in Israel, and knowest not these things?"

In the second place, if he does not teach this truth, a teacher falls into the delusion of thinking that moral and religious instruction is all that is needed to uplift mankind. While moral and religious instructions are indispensable in the cultivation of Christian character, it is only through the new birth that Christian character can be begun. Christian character is the result of the Christian life, and Christian life is not possible apart from Christ: "For he that hath the Son hath life, and he that hath not the Son of God, hath not life." One may wash, cut, and polish diamonds so they will scintillate as they reflect the rays of the sun, but no one would plant them in the hope that he might produce *living* diamonds and thereby increase his wealth. No, it is not in man to save himself. He cannot be one of God's children unless he has been born again by the Spirit of God. Only so can he make spiritual progress and only so can he develop true Christian character.

In the third place, let any preacher know that when he preaches this cardinal truth he may have the keen satisfaction of knowing that he is preaching that which is intellectually acceptable in the most respected theological circles. Liberal theology repudiated the teaching of the new birth for several centuries, but in so doing, was quite off the track. This has been most tragically pointed up by Paul Tillich, Professor of Philosophical Theology at Harvard Divinity School, who summed up the theological situation in Europe in these words: "Neo-Protestantism is dead in Europe. All groups whether Lutheran, Reformed, or Barthian consider the last two hundred years of Protestant theology essentially erroneous." What a sad confession, but what does that mean in plain language? It means that liberal theology for two centuries had been talking about man's goodness, man's ability to evolve spiritually into a child of God without undergoing the radical process of regeneration, and, in so doing, had been most certainly teaching error. And who can estimate the evil that flowed from this erroneous theology?

Not long ago at Northfield, an address was delivered by Stanley High. As is known, Mr. High assisted President Eisenhower in the preparation of his campaign speeches. The subject of his address was: "Why the Church Has Failed Me." After confessing that he had failed the church, he turned the tables and gave his reasons why he felt the church had failed him. He said:

> The first business of the church is to redeem me. And I don't mean to redeem me in the purely social sense which convinces me that the Golden Rule ought to be my confession of faith. By redeeming me, I mean personal redemption, the process by which I am spiritually shaken apart and spiritually put together again, and from which I—the personal I—emerge a totally different person. . . . The reason for this failure is that the church, the modern modernist Protestant church, rates me altogether too highly. . . . I'm simply not as good as modern Protestantism assumes me to be. . . . Ever since my Sunday school days I had it dinned into my ears that I'm a child of God, and that I'm made in His image. It seems to me that those who lay so much emphasis on my bearing such a resemblance to the Almighty are not only

mistaken about me, they're also mistaken about history.
. . . The whole of the Bible and the whole of the ministry of Jesus, as I understand it, were designated not to
persuade man how good he is on his own, but how evil
he is on his own. And how good, by the process of redemption he can become. . . . I, personally, need the
church as I never needed it before. I happen to know
that my fellow laymen need it as never before and are
ready, at the slightest suggestion, to acknowledge that
need. . . . Its objective, so far as I am concerned, will not
be my cultivation, but my rebirth. I might fail that
kind of a church, but that kind of a church could not
fail me.

And this is the kind of a church we need today. When
the church teaches these truths, let it never be ashamed of
its testimony. In a day when our modern teachers confess
their inability to change men in their basic natures, let the
church proclaim the doctrine of the new birth, which doctrine alone deals factually with man, his deepest need and
his highest good. Only so will the church discharge its
highest responsibility. Those teachers of the church dedi-
cated to this Biblical emphasis are the truest pedagogues.
They are God's recruiting agents for the kingdom that has
no end, for a kingdom that cannot be moved, and by the
entrance into which men become heirs of eternal life. Christ,
the greatest of teachers, was principally an exponent of this
truth. Christ saw more deeply than any other into what man
was and what his basic needs are. May the church be found
faithful in presenting this truth, in the knowledge that in so
doing she renders a service to mankind second to none and
has, as her blessed end, the glory of our redeeming God.

J. LESTER HARNISH

Born in Nova Scotia, Canada.

A.B., D.D., Wheaton College; B.D., M.Th., Eastern Baptist Theological Seminary.

Pastor, Euclid Baptist Church, Brooklyn, New York; Belmont Avenue Baptist Church, Philadelphia; Bethel Baptist Church, Detroit, Michigan; Temple Baptist Church, Los Angeles, California.

Trustee, California Baptist Theological Seminary, Covina, California; member, Board of Directors of Los Angeles Baptist City Mission Society; member, Executive Committee, Southern California Baptist State Convention.

Contributing editor, *Seek* (devotional magazine); correspondent, *Christianity Today.*

The Mechanics Employed

THE PREACHERS OF NEW TESTAMENT TIMES proclaimed Christ incarnate, crucified, risen, and coming again. This kerygma was effective. Why? Obviously, their personal experience with Christ, the power of the Holy Spirit, and the depth of their consecration accounted for their effectiveness. For example, Paul was conscious of a great call as an apostle to challenge the will, as a prophet to probe the conscience, as an evangelist to woo the heart, as a pastor to care for the soul, as a teacher to inform the mind. But removed by two thousand years, we wonder about the mechanics employed in communicating the Gospel. How did they prepare sermons? We can conjecture the preparation involved. They had personal preparation, certain limited resource reading, a knowledge of the audience to which they spoke and the Word of God which they preached. Today these same essentials must be observed.

PERSONAL PREPARATION

Apostolic sermons were prepared by men who had been in the school of Jesus. We are living in an age when academic preparation is required of the man who feels called to preach the Good News. Four years of college and three years of seminary is but the beginning—the forging of tools to be burnished and sharpened with use and increasing skill. Graduate work? Yes, if possible, but more important, continued personal growth so that we grow in the likeness of Christ. The days of preparation never end. Great and exacting discipline must be stringently exercised to keep from professionalism, laziness, pride, carelessness, distracting mannerisms and weaknesses. The church of Jesus Christ rises or falls according to the ideals and application of those who are set apart for the office of prophet. The daily devotional life, study habits, and personal purity are necessary in the preparation of a sermon.

Physical discipline is an integral part of sermon preparation. Late rising, inadequate diet, and flabby muscles make for a sluggish mind. A secluded and private room, where distractions and interruptions will be at a minimum, will help make effective sermon preparation possible.

RESOURCES

We are on a par with Peter and Paul as to the great Resource—the Holy Spirit. We have His presence. We can have His power. Though their written material, other than the Old Testament, was sparse and precious, we have the New Testament, plus an unlimited supply of Biblical literature. Our sermons are only as worthwhile as we are personally endued with the power of the Holy Spirit, saturated with the Word of God and the wisdom of great minds. We must be completely dissatisfied with anything less than the Holy Spirit's presence and power, but we must also be bookworms. How easy it is for most of us to pursue routine pastoral duties and to absent ourselves from the study—the place where God and man commune!

In the study there should be a fine library costing at least as much as the car we drive. Emphasis should be placed upon resource books, not books of sermons. Bible encyclopedias, dictionaries, lexicons, and commentaries should comprise the largest section. Most of us also have access to the libraries of the city and educational institutions including seminaries and Bible schools. But books are of no value unless used regularly. Five days per week, four hours a day should be the minimum time spent in concentrated reading and disciplined study. The longer we stay in a community, the greater the pressure is to neglect this well-spring. The result is to "run dry" in the pulpit, causing pastors to move frequently from one charge to another.

In the study should be certain aids that make the books and other materials usable. An alphabetized topical file of illustrations deserves a whole filing cabinet which can be fed by wide range of reading, clipping, classifying, and filing. Every sermon should be filed after it is carefully coded, recorded, and cross-filed in a card index which gives the title, text, subject, and type of the sermon. Of course this record should indicate the place and date of delivery. It also helps to keep a chronological tabulation of all sermons, addresses, and talks so as to avoid the embarrassment of repetition should one give a message under similar circumstances.

THE AUDIENCE

How shall we know what to preach? We are commissioned

to cry but one message—the Word of God. What we deliver will be determined by the need of the people to whom we speak. Seldom should we preach the sermon we like. It was not easy for Isaiah to preach, "All flesh is as grass," or for John to condemn Herod's infidelity, or for Paul to tell the Athenians that they were religious but lost, or for Jesus to confront the spiritual leaders of His day with the demand that they be born again. In every case the need determined the message. Let us observe as much as possible our charges in their homes, at work, in community activities, at school, or on the world scene. Then in the quiet of the study, on our knees with the Word of God open before us, ask, "Holy Father, what wilt *Thou* have me to proclaim?"

In the light of the above, I often find it difficult to say in one sermon anything adequate. So, rather than try to rush or prolong a series of sermons on the general subject, I deliver each sermon having its own topic under which a phrase of the general subject is treated. I know of no other way to deal with such tremendous themes as missions, evangelism, the second coming, etc. For example: *Burning Questions About the Founder of Christianity:* (1) Who Was Jesus and Why Did He Come?; (2) What Is a Christian?; (3) What Alternative Does Christ Offer?; (4) What Right Does Christ Have To Be the Redeemer?; (5) Is Christ's Cross Necessary?; (6) Is There a Resurrection of the Dead?; (7) What Must You Do With Jesus?; (8) Techniques of the Resurrection; (9) What Does Christ Do for the Believer in the Present Life? *What About These Cults?:* (1) Mormonism; (2) Unity; (3) Jehovah's Witnesses; (4) Christian Science. *Christ Is the Answer:* (1) For the Aged; (2) For Mothers; (3) For Bachelors and Fathers; (4) For Lovers; (5) For Those Who Mourn; (6) For the Teen-ager; (7) For the Devil; (8) For Newlyweds. *The Demands of Christ:* (1) Follow Me; (2) Take Up Your Cross!; (3) Cut It Off!; (4)

Love Your Enemies; (5) Do Not Be Anxious; (6) Have
Faith in God; (7) Believe in Me; (8) Be Perfect.

It is helpful to synchronize one's preaching with the season
of the year. While the nation's attention is focused on July
4, why not preach a sermon on some allied patriotic theme?
Instead of preaching one sermon on Christmas Sunday morning on the advent of Christ, why not use all of December to
exalt Immanuel? The merchants now stretch the Christmas
buying season to several weeks. So while this spirit is in the
air, why not take advantage of it?

Frequently a series of helpful messages should be delivered
for those who are going through common experiences of life,
such as loneliness, discouragement, sorrow, trouble, worry,
and sickness. Periodically community and world problems
should be dealt with, such as juvenile delinquency, divorce,
alcoholism, separation of Church and State, Christian life-
service, integration, ecumenicity. Sermons that do not live
where people walk are not worth preparing, let alone hearing. Let me be very careful to point out emphatically that
each sermon must be thoroughly Biblical (saturated with
the Word of God) and Christ-exalting. Sometimes your audience will be community, service, or cultural clubs composed
of leading citizens. Adapt the form of the sermon but never
alter the contents. You have been invited to speak as a minister of Jesus Christ—be true to your calling and don't betray
the trust of those who called you.

MATERIAL

The apostles proclaimed the Old Testament and that
which the Holy Spirit revealed to them. We are under solemn obligation to proclaim the whole Word of God as we are
led by the Holy Spirit. Textual and expository preaching are
the procedures which best accomplish this. Having prepared
himself spiritually, physically, and mentally, and having ascer-

tained the needs of his audience, the sermonic craftsman uses his every resource to exalt God's Word.

In the light of the occasion a verse or passage is prayerfully chosen weeks or months in advance of the preaching date. A folder is then set up for that one sermon. Into the folder is casually placed material that can be gleaned from the pastor's files, library, or current reading, be it Biblical or otherwise. During the week preceding the date when the sermon is to be delivered, two days are set aside to reread, survey, evaluate, eliminate, and arrange all the material that has been collected in the folder. I first write out the conclusion, then number the material in logical sequence, which leads up to the conclusion.

An outline emerges which is too long or wordy. After further refining, two to five points will stand out. Others will be used as subpoints or discarded. At this point I construct an attention-demanding (I hope) introduction designed to start right where the minds of most of the audience are, thence to pursue relentlessly to the conlcusion, which is usually twenty-five minutes away. The last things added are illustrations. If these do not come from actual life, preferably that of the speaker or his audience, they are best omitted. Skillful, sincere use of the illustrations enhances the sermon's effectiveness immeasurably. It is not unusual for a listener to remember a story and its point when the masterpiece of a sermon is long since forgotten. Only employ illustrations to clarify, beautify, verify, and vivify a truth.

My notes are reduced to a sheet of paper, 8½″ x 11″, folded across the middle and turned so as to fit conveniently into my Bible. The notes will be four pages or less. These notes are handwritten in four colors of ink, providing a scheme which my eye can catch quickly. They are completed by Friday noon and literally live with me wherever I go until we enter the pulpit Sunday as old friends.

In the last ten years I have employed a procedure that has

been well received and most beneficial. Though I disclaim originality, I do not know to whom credit is due. No doubt many have used the Book-of-the-Week plan. Every church needs a comprehensive knowledge of the Bible. Many church members who have intended to read the Bible through completely do not do it. Why not sign them up for membership in a Book-of-the-Week Club? Capitalize on their guilt complex and their American weakness as "joiners." Have them agree to read a book of the Bible each week. At the midweek service distribute a brief mimeographed outline containing the key word, key verse, date, author, introduction, popular outline, and memory verse. Teach from this. Loose-leaf notebook covers of appropriate size should be available at cost. On Sunday morning the pastor's sermon is entitled, "The Message of Genesis" or something better worded in which he lucidly places before the congregation the one great theme of that book. This takes much thought and preparation, but every book in the Bible can be reduced to one pre-eminent living message. In the evening an evangelistic text is taken from the same book, and the quest for souls is on. Biblical knowledge, interest, attendance, and spiritual fruitage will result. The same can be done with a single book of the Bible, taking a chapter or portion per week. The basic doctrines of the faith can be handled this same way. This procedure will help overcome the spiritual and Biblical illiteracy found in the average local church.

I find it helpful in many ways to record all sermons which I deliver in the church which I am now serving. From these, four sermons are transcribed each month, laboriously edited (a humiliating and corrective task!), made available in mimeographed or printed form at cost. It is good discipline in point of length of time consumed in delivery as well as self-criticism. A wider ministry is made possible. If ever you are misquoted, recorded proof can be produced in your defense.

Somewhere I read that as a young man Alexander Maclaren, of Manchester, helped in the application of himself to the task of sermon preparation by donning a military cloak and helmet. Then, with an old sword which had been lying on the desk, he would marshal his forces with stout heart and stubborn resolve to storm the bastions of truth determined to carry off victoriously the greatest treasures. May our heavenly Father grant that His Holy Spirit will lead you into all truth as you marshal your God-given forces to proclaim the unsearchable riches of the grace of our Lord Jesus Christ.

Your Greatest Privilege

Text: Proverbs 3:1, 2; Ephesians 4:32

J. Lester Harnish

THE KINDNESS OF ANIMALS is well known to all. Just a week ago the press carried a story about two dogs in a certain neighborhood. One was a homeless, mangy, blind mongrel. The other one was a thoroughbred that had a very good home. Each day the favored dog would go to a neighbor's house, pick up some food (usually a bone) and carry it back and place it before the blind dog. That is how the unfortunate one continued to live. I also read of a bird that was found in a tree. In spite of the fact that it had been there for many days, it was not thin and emaciated, because other birds had fed it. The eagle catches its young on its wings and bears them out over the cliff. The bear boxes its cubs to get them ready for the reality of life in the woods. The partridge fakes a broken wing and leads the hunter away from the nest. Animals can be kind. But it takes terrific effort for man to be kind. He is not born with kindness in him.

By kindness we mean that high sense of consideration for others that results in helping, even if it costs something. It is not hard to recall those in our lives who have either gripped us or griped us. It is easy to remember in a lifetime acts of kindness for there are not too many of them. One of my earliest recollections of real downright kindness happened on one cold, blowy, wintry night when my dad was trying to

71

get home from work in our little village in Canada. His Model T Ford got stuck in the mountainous snows. A Negro helped him get the car home. My father took off his own hands a pair of double-knitted mittens and gave them to the Negro who had none. I must have been six years old at that time, yet it is indelibly impressed on my memory. I well remember the short, roly-poly choir director who first asked me to sing in the choir. I remember the nationally known Bible teacher who helped me to dream of the possibility of going to college, and when I arrived I found that he had placed on deposit a sum of money that was to be credited to my account. How very rare! How long has it been since you have seen someone conduct a dear old lady across the street or help a blind person?

Our difficulty seems to be that we do not trust people. Usually we live on the defensive. Our mortal enemies are those who serve us—the policeman, the waitress, the clerk. We do not give them a chance to be kind, and usually we are anything but kind to them. We act as though our home circle were a prize ring, where continual fighting goes on, rather than kindness. Yet of all of God's creatures we Christians should be the kindest. There is a direct command of the Holy Spirit by the pen of Paul: "Be ye kind one to another, tenderhearted, forgiving one another, even as God for Christ's sake hath forgiven you" (Eph. 4:32). This is our greatest privilege.

The greatest indictment that Jesus had against the religionists of His day was their lack of kindness. In Luke 13, Jesus was preaching in a synagogue. In the midst of His sermon, He stopped everything to show kindness to some-one! Two thousand years later we find ourselves so caught up in the discharge of our religious duties that we find it hard to be kind. Jesus was trying to say, by that act, that what He was doing by way of kindness was more important than what He was saying. The Pharisees had gotten so far away from the spirit of God that they, though they were keeping the letter of the Law, had evidently lost the capacity for being kind. Yet this is man's greatest privilege.

I. Kindness Is an Asset to the Kingdom of God

It is our greatest privilege first because kindness has always been an asset to the kingdom of God. In the early church its first and greatest strength was obviously the power of the Holy Spirit.

Their second source of strength was not a creed or an organization but kindness. Listen to II Corinthians 6:6: "By pureness, by knowledge, by longsuffering, *by kindness,* by the Holy Ghost, love unfeigned." Our means of entree into the hearts of people as the Holy Spirit prepares the way is by acts of kindness. I have a hunch that is why Paul never gave up making tents. Paul told the Christians at Rome (Rom. 15:1, 2) that they ought to be kind to each other, to bear the infirmities of the weak and not please themselves. This doesn't mean that we are to be busybodies, professional do-gooders. We should be helpful to those who deserve it the least. Yes, folks are ungrateful and even downright spiteful. Yet Paul wrote in I Corinthians 13, "Love suffereth long and is kind." The greatest kindness to which we can point and from which our kindness should spring is Calvary. "While we were yet sinners [when we deserved no kindness at all], Christ died for the ungodly" (Rom. 5:6). Scripture we did memorize, church services we did attend, and we did tithe, but what of the cup of cold water, the visit to the person in need, the crust of bread? Kindness is what will separate the "sheep and the goats," the blessed and the condemned. Kindness has always been an asset in the kingdom of God.

II. Kindness Kindles Hope

The kind word that was spoken by the teacher to the problem boy in the class was what helped him to do better work. The kind deed that was done by the boss to help the slow worker is what made him a better employee. The kindness that was shown the sinner is what contributed to bring him into the kingdom. When a self-righteous crowd brought before Jesus a woman of sin, He could have drawn Himself up in His infinite purity and scornfully poured condemnation on the poor woman. But He knew that she needed kindness. "Let him that is without sin cast the first stone." After they had left, He turned and said, "Woman, where are thine accusers? Neither do I condemn thee. Go and sin no more." It kindled great hope in her life. Jesus was so busy. Yet He had time to be kind. We are so busy that we become matter-of-fact, brusque, caustic, and even selfish. But we leave in our wake bruised feelings, discouraged spirits, and frustrated personalities. By a word of kindness we can kindle hope in the anxious, the weary, the unlovely, those who lack confidence, the lonely, the fearful, and the apathetic.

The story is told by F. H. Hadley who, for so many years, was the beloved director of the old Water Street Mission in the Bowery of New York. Major had not drawn a sober breath in years. Characteristically, when the invitation was given, Major would stagger down the aisle toward the altar rail, kneel unsteadily, and go into the next room and receive a bowl of soup and a bed. One night Hadley's patience was at an end. He met the Major halfway in the aisle, turned him around and pushed him out of the door into the cold, dark night. But when Hadley went home he could not sleep. He finally lost the battle with his conscience and his Lord and at two o'clock in the morning he got up and got dressed and started looking for the Major. He was well-known in the Bowery and it took only a very short time to find him in a back room, lying in some dirty sawdust, sound asleep in a drunken stupor. Hadley sat down alongside and picking up the Major's head, pushed back the dirty hair. As he did so, Major stirred. Hadley said, "Major, I want you to know that Jesus loves you and I try. If you will come back to the mission, we will give you a bowl of soup and a bed." Major struggled to a sitting position and said, "What was that you said?" Hadley said, "If you will come back to the mission, we will give you something to eat and put you to bed." "No, no, what was it you said first?" Hadley said, "Jesus loves you and I am trying to." Whereupon Major broke down, tears came to his eyes and he sobbed, "That's the first time that has been said to me since my little daughter was killed fifteen years ago by an automobile and I took to drink." Hadley took the Major back, cleaned him up, and put him to bed. The next day the Major made a sober decision for Jesus Christ and by the transforming grace of the Gospel never took another drink. He died six months later but during those months, the old Major was a great worker for God, helping to win hundreds to Jesus. All because of the kindness of a man. This is more than our hymn singing and our theological creed. Kindness is to be found in deed.

> When a man ain't got a cent and he's feeling kind of
>   blue
> An' the clouds hang dark an' heavy, an' won't let the
>   sunshine through,
> It's a great thing, O, my brethren, for a feller just to lay
> His hand upon your shoulder, in a friendly sort o' way!

So sang James Whitcomb Riley. If the Christian has not experienced the kindness of God, he has never become a Christian. If, in turn, the Christian does not give some evidence of at least a desire to be kind, how dwells the love of God in that man? For when we were without hope, Christ died for us. Or as Nehemiah put it, "God is slow to anger and of great kindness" (9:17).

III. KINDNESS PAYS OFF

But lastly, kindness is not only an asset in the kingdom of

God, not only does it kindle hope, but it pays off. Kindness will never cause regret.

> I have wept in the night
>   For the shortness of sight
> that to somebody's need made me blind!
>   But I never have yet
>   Felt a twinge of regret
> for being a little too kind.

In the pastor's instruction class we study the church covenant, the last part of which is very practical, dealing with our relationship with each other as Christians. One of the subjects covered is gossiping. I urge that we ask three questions before gossip. Is it true? Is it necessary? Is it kind? Let us practice the Golden Rule.

Kindness is always a source of good will. We spend billions of dollars for defense. Yet these weapons do not pay off as well as do lend-lease, the Point Four Program, the International Red Cross, the Christian missionary program, we believe. Let us wage an amazing war of kindness. Let us help people to have better food, housing, health, and be able to read and write.

It engenders good will at home, too. I am afraid some of us parents are like chill, winter winds that blow through our homes. driving our children into warmer climates. But, thank God, some are just like gay bands that will light up a whole neighborhood with the lilt of the music of their lives. You bring happiness as you share your kindness with others. Some of you are like our groves at orange blossom time, when sweet fragrance is spread over whole sections of our county.

Peter was thinking of our homes when he was trying to instruct the believers of his day to be better Christians. He lists desirable qualities, then says, "Add to your godliness, brotherly kindness" (II Peter 1:7). In the home we often fail at that point. We are so religious and righteous that we forget to be kind. That was the weakness of Puritanism.

We are on a two-way street. The lack of kindness to parents by today's children is altogether too obvious. Today's children are not worse than previous generations. I want to be a friend of the youth. I want them to know that I believe in them and want to help them. But children must be kind as well as parents. Not long ago I conducted a funeral service for a very aged gentleman who had six children, fifteen grandchildren and seven great-grandchildren. Most of them lived on the West Coast. At the service, *one* of his children was present and one grandchild. There were three floral pieces. That was all.

One of our national scandals is the failure of today's children to care for their aged parents. They commit their aged parents to the institutions. We have no way of taking care of the senile in the State of California under our present laws, unless they are committed to the institutions for the insane, but the aged ones are not insane. They are weak with age and they need love, kindness, and attention.

I thank God for a person who said to me the other day, "I am afraid that I will have to cut down a little bit in my church activities because I think it is going to be necessary in the foreseeable future to bring Mother into our home." Whereupon I said, "I want you to know that I am all for that. It is far better for you to fulfill Scripture, which tells us that we are worse than the heathen if we do not take care of our own, in showing kindness to your aged mother than to be chairman of the board in Temple Baptist Church." Of course, there are times when circumstances dictate institutionalizing of the patient. But when our loved ones are old they need love and kindness. As Christians, this is our responsibility.

IV. CONCLUSION

Kindness is something we all can have and share, for it is simple, uncluttered, and uncomplicated. When Jesus was walking through Jericho, remember when He looked and saw a tax collector in a sycamore tree. Jesus stood for all that was right and pure and honest and trustworthy. Jesus had every right to say, "You son of a devil. You come down here," and proceed to heap invectives upon him. But Jesus saved His harshness for self-styled saints. Instead of condemning Zacchaeus, He said, "Zacchaeus, let's have supper together tonight." Zacchaeus was taken completely off guard. Before the evening was over, Zacchaeus heard himself saying, in response to this kindness, "I give back everything that I have taken unjustly, and I will restore it many fold."

Do you remember the story of Thomas Carlyle? Two famous American authors came one day and sat down with him just to hear him elucidate out of his great fund of wisdom. For one solid hour, Carlyle spoke on one subject after another. Finally out of sheer exhaustion he stopped long enough to catch his breath. Silence reigned. Nearby was his wife. She was the one who had quit her work and given up her career in order to lose herself in her beloved husband. She served him like a slave, without recompense. Hearing her labored breathing, impatiently Carlyle said, "Jane, for heaven's sake, don't breathe so loudly." It was a short time after that that she took ill and died. Looking through her personal effects, Carlyle found her diary in which she had spelled out her love and devotion for him. She had expected no recompense except love. But he had been so busy impressing the world with his talents that he had no time to share his affection. She had died of a broken heart—malnutrition of affection.

Carlyle went out that very day and started the first of daily pilgrimages to her graveside, where he would sit on the turf and rock himself in woe, saying, "Oh, Jane, if I had only known, if I had only known!" I sometimes wonder what went through the mind of Joseph of Arimathaea and Nicodemus when they came to the tomb. They had shown Jesus kindness, but after He died. Their kindness came too late. Is this true with us? Ought we not to go forth this morning as apostles of kindness? Kindness is our greatest privilege.

ROBERT G. LEE

Born in Fort Mill, South Carolina.

A.B., Furman University, 1913; Ph.D., Chicago Law School, 1919. Honorary degrees, D.D., LL.D., Litt.D., from Furman University, Stetson University, Baylor University, Howard-Payne College, Bob Jones University, Houghton College, and Union University.

Pastor, First Baptist Church, Edgefield, South Carolina; the First Baptist Church, Chester, South Carolina; the First Baptist Church, New Orleans, Louisiana; the Citadel Square Baptist Church, Charleston, South Carolina; and the Bellevue Baptist Church, Memphis, Tennessee, for past thirty years. President of the Southern Baptist Convention three terms; and president of the Tennessee Baptist State Convention four terms. Conference and radio preacher.

Author of twenty-three books and many pamphlets.

Forty-Seven Years

WITH NO FALSE MODESTY, I say in telling others my method of sermon preparation, I may seem to some far wiser than I as a candle telling full-blaze chandeliers how to shine, or like a chirping sparrow telling nightingales how to sing, or a trickling rill telling a river how to flow. Nevertheless, I tell how I have, for forty-seven years, made sermon preparations.

First of all, I go to the prayer closet and shut the door and ask God to guide me to the selection of a text and in my study and interpretation of any portion of the Scripture. I try to keep in mind the details of my commission authorizing me to speak from my pulpit for God—knowing that prayer in the study necessary for sermon preparation is as essential as steam for the locomotive to have power, as sap for the tree to be fruitful, and as blood for the body to be healthy. I pray much *before* I study. During my preparation, I pause occasionally to pray. I sometimes put down my pen and get down on my knees before God. Sometimes Scripture verses and an outline for a sermon on those verses come suddenly—in a minute or so. Then I set to work—remembering that what my need and the need of those to whom I am to speak is what God can do.

Second, I go to study, with no doubts about the Bible being the inspired Word of God. I believe and preach that "all scripture is given by inspiration of God" (II Tim. 3:16)—I believe that the whole Bible is supernatural in origin, divine in authorship, infallible in authority, infinite in scope, universal in interest, eternal in duration, inestimable in value, unequaled in simplicity of expression, regenerative in power, inspired in totality—the miracle Book of diversity in unity, of harmony in infinite complexity.

Believing that the Word of God is the Sword of the Spirit (Eph. 6:17), I do not give book reviews or speak on current events or on political matters—even though quotations from books and the bare mention of current events may be used. Believing that one purpose of preaching is to bring people to experience the new birth, I forget not that people are "born again, not of corruptible seed, but of incorruptible, by the word of God, which liveth and abideth forever" (I Peter 1:23). I do not forget that the entrance of God's Word gives light (Ps. 119:130).

Though I may use quotations and illustrations from many sources, I try never to substitute a "Thus saith the mind of man" for a "Thus saith the Lord."

Third, when I have chosen a portion of Scripture, whether

the portion be only part of a verse, or a verse, or many verses, I make sin my target, the salvation of the lost one my goal, the stirring of the saints to real soldiership in Christ's service an objective, and the comfort of the sad and heartbroken another objective. I hold in mind these words: "For the wages of sin is death, but the gift of God is eternal life through Jesus Christ our Lord" (Rom. 6:23).

I have no patience with those who administer laughing gas for the painless extraction of sin—because today nothing endangers spiritual values more than the easy-going attitude toward sin which prevails so widely. The Word of God tells us to hate evil—to shun every appearance of it. "Abhor that which is evil," admonished the apostle Paul (Rom. 12:9). I know that preachers should repeatedly tear away the disguise under which sin masquerades, should expose it as an opiate in the will, a frenzy in the imagination, a madness in the brain, a poison in the heart.

Knowing the solemnity of the preaching hour, many times I have reminded myself of some statement a great man has made as this one by Dr. Charles L. Goodell: "It is a great hour when a surgeon holds a scalpel at the end of which is life or death for the patient. It is a greater hour when a lawyer faces a jury, with the conviction that if he makes a mistake an innocent man will hang and a family be disgraced forever. But the greatest hour any human being ever faces is the hour when he stands before a man hastening to condemnation and is commissioned to offer him a pardon that is to last for the eternities."

In acknowledgment of this truth, I make preparation for preaching, determining never to minister "without blood in the bowl," having a verdict in mind as one fruit of the sermon.

Fourth, after I do much research work in history, in literature, in nature, in philosophy, in science, in biography, in botany, in astronomy, in poetry, and in other realms, I see if there are truths I have found to strengthen or illumine my sermon. Then I go into a sort of questioning of myself. I ask such questions as these: Am I clean before the Lord? God says: "Be ye clean, that bear the vessels of the Lord" (Isa. 52:11). As I must rebuke others, do I need rebuke? Am I willing to bear abuse for the message? Do I seek to please men or God? How much am I willing to count loss that the message may be gain to others? Am I really concerned about the unsaved? Am I really distressed about the sorrows of others? Is there any point of controversy between me and the Father over any one thing? Do I believe that one reservation cancels the act of consecration? Do I believe in Hell and Heaven as the Bible sets them forth? Do I practice what I preach? I often hold in mind these words: "Thou therefore which teachest another, teachest thou not thyself? thou that preachest a man should not steal, dost thou steal? Thou that sayest a man should not commit adultery, dost thou commit adultery? Thou that abhorrest idols, dost thou commit sacrilege? Thou that makest thy boast of the law, through breaking the law dishonorest thou God?" (Rom. 2:21-23).

Fifth, I remind myself that I am to speak *to* people and not just *before* people. Therefore, I seek to make the application of truth personal—as though I were talking face to face in private conversation. Spurgeon says, "Where the application begins, the sermon begins." That means, as I have read, that I must strive to make folks take to themselves what I say. Daniel Webster once said, and repeated it with emphasis, "When a man preaches to me, I want him to make it a personal matter, a personal matter, a personal matter." Of this, Dr. Broadus said: "And it is our solemn duty thus to address all men, whether they wish it or not." We must address men as directly as Moses spoke to King Pharaoh (Exod. 5:1), as Nathan spoke to David (II Sam. 12:1), as Elijah addressed Ahab (I Kings 18:18), as John the Baptist addressed King Herod (Mark 6:18), and as Paul thrust sharp and solemn words at Elymas, the sorcerer (Acts 13:10), and Felix (Acts 24:25).

In all of this, I remember that it is my business to persuade men, knowing myself the terror of the Lord (II Cor. 5:11).

Sixth, I sometimes feel led of God to choose some unusual texts without any desire to be spectacular, such as: "The Smoked Bottle" (Ps. 119:83). "Sitting on Doorknobs" (Jer. 17:11). "Chasing Fleas and Dead Dogs" (I Sam. 24:14). "Boo!" (Ezek. 25:3, 4). "Producers and Parasites" (Job 1: 14). Many of the follies of men and much Gospel truth can be set forth in the utilization of such verses.

Moreover, I have prepared and preached, to the salvation of many, sermons on "Runs of the Bible," "Weepings of the Bible," "Sleepings of the Bible," "Kisses of the Bible," "Laughter of the Bible," and such.

Chiefly, in all my sermon preparation and pulpit utterances, I exalt Christ, using texts from both the Old Testament and New Testament to do so, since Jesus is the theme of both.

The Old Testament conceals Jesus; the New Testament reveals Jesus.

The Old Testament prophesies Jesus; the New Testament produces Jesus.

The Old Testament promises Jesus; the New Testament presents Jesus.

My exaltation of Christ may be poorly done, but in all my preparation, I remember "that God hath highly exalted him and hath given him a name which is above every name" (Phil. 2:9). Every road of thought that does not lead to Jesus is apt to turn out to be a blind alley. One great thinker said: "God never thought, or said, or did anything except through Christ."

In so doing I believe that Jesus is worthy of all the praise that many and all superlative adjectives can give Him.

It may be worth little to all to know that I write my sermons with my own hand. Seldom do I dictate a sermon. After I write them, my secretary types them. Then, in preparation for their delivery, I read them over, picturize them (not memorize), and deliver them, usually without notes before me.

And in my delivery I ask God to give me genuine earnestness and passion. It was written of Demosthenes that sometimes he spoke with such passionate earnestness that his enemies said he was deranged. But people listened to him like children frightened at the roar of a storm, or like slaves to an emancipation proclamation.

Whether any of my way of sermon preparation is to be commended or followed, I know not. But this is my method: I venture to give to you.

Christ Above All

Robert G. Lee

He that cometh from above is above all . . . he that cometh from heaven is above all— (John 3:31) .

THESE WORDS are from John the Baptist, the friend of the Bridegroom—entrusted with the delicate and sacred responsibility of interpreting the voice of betrothal. Nearly always did John the Baptist speak in judicial tones; and his words were sharp arrows that pierced the hearts of prating formalists, artful hypocrites, political tricksters, skeptical Sadducees, and gross materialists. In preaching, John asked for a verdict and got it in repentant decisions followed by baptism. John bore no credentials from the learned rabbis and exhibited no diploma from the schools of the prophets. While he descended upon the iniquities of his day with a torch in one hand and a sword in the other, he pointed out Jesus as the Lamb of God, baptized Jesus with the approval of Heaven, and said of Jesus, "He that cometh from above is above all."

Now he who sets mind, heart, tongue, and hand with pen to set forth the wonders and worth of Jesus, Son of man without sin and Son of God with power, sets himself to a task that puts men and angels to an eternal nonplus.

Though much of Christ be unfolded in one age by profound thinkers and more revealed in another age by the wisest on earth and by the angels in Heaven, yet eternity itself cannot suffice fully to unfold Him.

A woeful sense of inadequacy oppresses us in all attempts to set forth the excellencies he has in himself and the treasures of righteousness in the blood of Him "who of God is made unto us wisdom, righteousness, sanctification, and redemption" (I Cor. 1:30).

Can a musician play Beethoven's Ninth Symphony on a tin whistle? Can a candle shine with the brilliance of the sun? Can one bowl of water cleanse one million dirty hands? No! And no more can human language compass the glory of the character of Christ whose life on this earth was an episode between two eternities—one reaching back before all worlds, the other forward forever.

Who, with the weightiest words of all languages most skillfully combined, most wisely written, and most eloquently spoken, can fully describe Him who was so finely strung, so unutterably keyed to truth, mercy, justice, love—who so quickly felt the sorrow, the sympathy, and the indignation which wrong and injustice invariably elicit from all high souls?

Jesus, whose name sounds down the corridors of the centuries like the music of all choirs poured forth in one anthem, is literature's loftiest ideal, philosophy's highest personality, criticism's supremest problem, theology's fundamental doctrine, spiritual religion's cardinal necessity. Religiously, socially, politically, economically, educationally, scientifically, nationally, and internationally Jesus is the only hope of our body-weary, head-dizzy, soul-sick, sin-smitten, war-scarred world.

Who am I to portray the Christ who is Heaven's bread for earth's hunger, Heaven's water for earth's thirst, Heaven's light for earth's death—when the most magnificent ceremonies assemble the people under the influence of His name?

> O, who can paint Him? Let the sweetest tone
> That ever trembled on the harps of heaven,

Be discord. Let the enchanting seraphim
Whose anthem is eternity, be dumb.
For praise and wonder, adoration, all
Melt into muteness ere they soar to Thee,
The sole Perfection, Theme of countless worlds!

I. CHRIST JESUS IS ABOVE ALL AS TO HIS SOURCE

He "had glory with God before the world was and was loved by the Father before the foundation of the world" (John 17). By the Father—the fountain, the ocean, the center of all delights and joys—Jesus was embraced from all eternity.

Jesus said: "The Father and I are one." And no child was ever so one with its mother, no wife ever so one with the husband of her heart, no husband ever so one with the wife of his bosom, no soul ever so one with the body as was Jesus with God in the glory He had with God before the world was (John 17).

No crystal streams flow so purely from stainless fountains, no beams of light come so unmixed from the sun, no fragrance issues so sweetly from flowers as did the delights from the holy, holy, holy Father's heart in embrace with the thrice-holy Son—in glory they had with each other before this world was.

II. JESUS CHRIST IS ABOVE ALL IN HIS RELATION TO CREATION

All things were made by him; and without him was not anything made that was made (John 1:3).

By him were all things created, that are in heaven, and that are in earth, visible and invisible, whether they be thrones, or dominions, or principalities, or powers: all things were created by him, and for him (Col. 1:16).

God . . . hath . . . spoken unto us by his Son . . . by whom also he made the worlds (Heb. 1:1, 2).

Creation in concept is the product of His wisdom. Creation in perfection is the product of His power. And today Jesus, the creating power, is at the center, the circumference, as well as all intervening space—upholding all things by the word of His power.

Who poured out from the crystal chalices of eternity the Amazon? the Po? the Rhine? the Mississippi? Who fringed the first flowers with His glory? Who took clots of the sun's blood and turned them into diamonds? Who planted the full moon like a huge jonquil in the garden of the stars? Who sent out the first ray of light like some flaming archangel with garments afire across the uncharted dark? Who set the sun in His tabernacle in the heavens? Who made the blades of grass emerald strings on which the soft fingers of the South wind play resurrection melodies? Who, night by night, lights His great world-house with planet lamps and star flambeaus? Who put the song in the throat of the mocking bird, the feathered Beethoven of the boughs? Who put the song in the throat of the lark, the Mendelssohn of the meadows? Who made all things?

One name answers all these questions—*Jesus.*

III. Christ Jesus Is Above All in the Way in Which He Made Entrance into the World

In eternity, Jesus Christ rested on the bosom of the Father without a mother! In time, He rested on the bosom of a mother without an earthly father.

An uncreated, divine Person, who had eternal pre-existence, He took the form of a created being and became in time what He was not in eternity—flesh. He was the great Creator born of the creature woman.

God who in Eden brought a motherless woman from the body of a man, in Bethlehem's barn brought a fatherless Man from the body of a woman. And Jesus, the Ancient of Days, became the Infant of days.

Did you ever hear of a baby just as old as his father? Jesus was just as old as His heavenly Father—co-equal, co-existent, co-eternal, and co-essential with the Father.

Did you ever hear of a boy one hundred years older than his mother? Jesus was ages older than Mary, the virgin mother.

Jesus who made man was made in the likeness of man. Jesus who created angels was made "a little lower than the angels." Jesus, who was before Abraham, was born two thousand years after Abraham. Jesus who was David's Lord became David's Son. Jesus who made all flesh was "made flesh." When was He "made flesh"? In that holy time when a Jewish virgin who had never known a man went down into that mysterious land of motherhood and came back holding in her arms the only Baby who never had an earthly father. And His every muscle was a pulley divinely swung, His every nerve divine handwriting, His every bone divine sculpture, His every heart beat divine pulsation, His every breath the breath of deity. He was God's will, God's thought, God's purpose swathed in mortality . He was the Light—God seen! He was the Word—God heard! He was the Life—God felt.

Milton had it right, who wrote:

> That glorious form, that light insufferable,
> That far-beaming blaze of majesty
> Wherewith he wont at Heaven's high council table to sit;
> The midst of Tribal unity,
> He laid aside—and here, with us to be,
> Forsook the courts of everlasting day
> And chose with us a darksome house of clay.

IV. CHRIST JESUS IS ABOVE ALL AS TO HIS REVELATION OF GOD

No man hath seen God at any time; the only begotten Son, which is in the bosom of the Father, he hath declared him (John 1:18) .

Jesus said: "He that hath seen me hath seen the Father" (John 14). Whoever reveals God must be God. Jesus expressed the entire being of God with entire precision, finality, and perfection. In Him the silence of God breaks into full voice.

To know Jesus is to know God. What Jesus was to prodigal and publican, to mother and child, to harlot and hypocrite, to saint and sinner, to rich and poor, to devils and disciples, that is God always, everywhere, to all people.

Jesus was the mind of God thinking out; Jesus was the heart of God throbbing out; the hand of God reaching out; the feet of God walking out; the eyes of God looking out; the ears of God listening out; the Person of God in human clothes.

Being God, He is God eternally, without cause, without beginning, without mutation, beyond measure, and without end. No other being, other than God, can claim equality with Jesus Christ. He is God above all, in all, through all— the Almighty.

As one has written, Christ expressed "the friendly affinity of fatherly authority; the devout integrity of divine immutability; the generous legacy of glorious liberality; the humble courtesy of holy constancy; the manifold ministry of majestic mercy; the wealthy sympathy of worthy sublimity; the healthy sanctity of heavenly sincerity; the manifest majesty of mediative mystery."

V. Christ Jesus Is Above All in His Supernatural Power

In power He is above and beyond the forces and facts of nature as a river is beyond a rill in reach.

Jesus never met a blind man to whom He did not give sight, or a dumb man He did not make speak, or a leper He did not cleanse, or a cripple He did not make walk, or a storm He did not calm.

Jesus never met a demon-possessed man He did not rid of the demons, or an outcast woman He did not lift up and put back in the path of virtue, or a crazy man He did not restore to reason, or a funeral procession, He did not break up.

Jesus, miracle above and beyond all His miracles, is the undeniable testimony to the truth that all power was and is His in Heaven and in earth.

Christ is no bell-hop running up and down the corridors of His world-hotel, having lost the keys to some of the doors. Christ is no superannuated butler in His own world-house. He is no law-limited Christ. To Him all power in earth and Heaven is given.

VI. CHRIST JESUS IS ABOVE ALL IN HIS TEACHING

Teacher of teachers, Jesus!

"Never man spake like this man." Read the doctrines of Plato, Socrates, Aristotle. You feel the difference between their words and Christ's is the difference between inquiry and declaration, between speculation and revelation, between surmise and certainty, between groping and guidance.

In boldness of conception, grandeur of character, sublimity of purpose, originality of mind, valiant propagandism, His teachings claim the sovereignty of the world.

Today, when the air is troubled with doubts, thick with negations that have no missions, no adventures, no beneficent audacities, we need to examine His teachings. "His teachings spurn the established boundaries of His day. They leap across conventional gulfs, across the deep chasms which yawn between race and race, between class and mass. All races and people are of equal sacredness. Character is more important than talent. Responsibility is measured according to endowment. Neighborliness is to be defined by the circle of necessity."

VII. CHRIST JESUS IS ABOVE ALL IN HIS SACRIFICIAL
     SUFFERING

"Christ our passover is sacrificed for us" (I Cor. 5:7).

Great is the Gospel of Christ's revealing truth, saving power, and condescending comradeship. But greater is the Gospel of His measureless sacrifice.

Jesus was perfect man and holy God in one Person. But there was more than the human nature in Christ that suffered. Had it been no more than His human nature which suffered, He would have suffered only finite suffering. If only the human nature of Jesus suffered, and suffered only a short time, we cannot say that His sufferings were infinite.

And if His sufferings were not infinite, they could not be a satisfaction for our sins, which sins demand infinite suffering.

If the divine nature did not suffer in its union with the human nature, then a suffering Saviour is no revelation of the nature of God.

If only the human nature suffered, and that suffering was not participated in by the divine nature, we have an infinite debt of sin canceled by finite suffering, which is absurd.

With only a *finite* price paid, our salvation cannot merit end-renown.

> For he hath made him to be sin for us, who knew
> no sin; that we might be made the righteousness of God
> in him (II Cor. 5:21).

That means that when Christ was sacrificed for us, God ordered sin to execution in the Person of His own Son, dealt with Jesus as He must deal with sin, in severe and unrelenting judgment.

In that supreme sacrifice, Jesus became for us all that God must judge, that we through faith in Him, can become all that God cannot judge.

VIII. CHRIST JESUS IS ABOVE ALL IN HIS RELATION TO DEATH

"Christ died." "Christ was buried." "Christ rose from the dead."

Yes, "Christ was buried." The kingdom about which He had talked had shrunk to the narrow dimensions of a grave. The regal robes they had hoped to see Him wear were now a shroud. The throne they had hoped to see Him occupy had disappeared in a tomb. His only scepter was a weed. His only crown was a crown of thorns. His only coronation acclamation was the spit they flung through sneering lips. His only throne was a cross. His only emblem of royal insignia was the marks of the scourge upon His naked back. His only inaugural speech was a lonely cry. His only glory was shame. His only coronation companions were two thieves. His only inaugural splendor was the black darkness that shrouded the world. His only king's cup was the sponge filled with vinegar and gall. His only authority was His failure to come down from the cross.

Death, whose only flowers are faded garlands on coffin lids, had trampled into lifeless dust the Rose of Sharon. Death, whose only music is the sob of broken hearts, had padlocked the mouth that so comfortingly had spoken to the sad. Death, whose only pleasure fountains are the falling tears of the world, had closed the eyes of Him who wept over Jerusalem. Death, with skeleton hand, had written "Ichabod" on all His claims. He arose—"arose a victor from the dark domain." And if Christ be not risen our preaching is vain, our faith is vain, we are false witnesses of God, we are yet in our sins, our departed loved ones who believed in Christ are perished.

But if there be no risen Christ, death mocks our hopes like a coarse comedian or a heartless satirist. No risen Christ, the whole history of Christianity and its existence is unintelligible. No risen Christ, the whole earth in deepest mourning dressed will, like Rachel of old, go down to the judgment weeping for her children, finding no comfort.

IX. CHRIST JESUS IS ABOVE ALL AS TO HIS PROMISED RETURN

> I will come again (John 14:3).

> The Son of man cometh at an hour when ye think not (Luke 12:40).

> This same Jesus . . . shall so come in like manner as ye have seen him go into heaven (Acts 1:11).

And Paul, by the Holy Spirit, wrote:

> For the Lord himself shall descend from heaven with a shout, with the voice of the archangel, and with the trump of God: and the dead in Christ shall rise first: then we which are alive and remain shall be caught up together with them in the clouds, to meet the Lord in the air: and so shall we ever be with the Lord. Wherefore comfort one another with these words (I Thess. 4:16-18).

And when Jesus comes back, His second advent will be the watchman's looked-for day, the husbandman's harvest day, the builder's completion day, the master's reckoning day, the servant's payday, the bride's wedding day, the king's coronation day.

"Amen! Even so, come, Lord Jesus."

And now—let me ask you some questions.

Where have you placed this glorious Christ whom God hath highly exalted and to whom God háth given a name above every name? Have you given highest place? Are you putting your family, business, pleasure, personal ambition, friends, or *yourself* ahead of Him? Are you letting anybody or anything keep you from giving Jesus highest place in your life?

Where do you place Jesus as to the use of your talents? And your time? Do you give Him minutes instead of hours? Hours instead of days? A year or so when you should give a lifetime?

Where do you place Jesus in your love? Where do you place Jesus as to the use of your body—through which you live and move and in which you have life? I beg you to heed this word:

> I beseech you, therefore, brethren, by the mercies of God, that ye present your bodies a living sacrifice, holy, acceptable unto God, which is your reasonable service (Rom. 12:1).

Let your thoughts of Christ urge you to be "always bearing about in the body the dying of the Lord Jesus, that the life also of Jesus might be made manifest in our body: for we which live are alway delivered unto death for Jesus' sake, that the life also of Jesus might be made manifest in our mortal flesh" (II Cor. 4:10, 11).

I ask you to make the voyage from the shallows to the deeps as set forth in the words:

> Oh, the bitter pain and sorrow
> That the time should ever be
> When my proud heart said to Jesus:
> "All of self and none of Thee."
>
> Still He sought me, I beheld Him
> Bleeding on the accursed tree,
> And my faint heart whispered softly:
> "Some of self and some of Thee."
>
> Day by day His tender mercy,
> Healing, helpful, full and free,
> Brought me lower, till I whispered:
> "Less of self and more of Thee."
>
> Higher than the highest heavens!
> Deeper than the deepest sea!
> Lord, thy love at last has conquered:
> "None of self and all of Thee."

Let me ask you to put Jesus above everything and everyone. Stick not to the transient things of this world—as one who prefers sound to substance.

Have no infatuation with this world—with its stagnant waters, its harps broken, its chalices cracked at dry wells, all its lands plowed with graves—until the One who is above all comes again or until His holy and pierced hands that opened to us the gates to grace shall open to us the gates to glory.

J. VERNON McGEE

Born in Hillsboro, Texas.

A.B., Southwestern University, Memphis, Tennessee, 1930; B.D., Columbia Theological Seminary, 1933; Th.M., Dallas Theological Seminary, 1937; Th.D., Dallas Theological Seminary, 1940; LL.D., John Brown University, 1952.

Pastor, Church of the Open Door since 1949. Prior to coming to this pastorate he served the Lincoln Avenue Presbyterian Church, Pasadena, California, for nine years. Dr. McGee also served in pastorates at Nashville, Tennessee and Cleburne, Texas.

Dr. McGee carries three weekly radio broadcasts and a daily "Hi-Noon Radio Bible Class," also a nightly Radio Bible Class— "Nine at Night." He also delivers annual lectures to the student body of Dallas Theological Seminary.

Author: *Ruth, The Romance of Redemption; Esther, The Romance of God's Providence; The Tabernacle, God's Portrait of Christ; Briefing the Bible; Going Through Genesis; Moving Through Matthew; The Prayer the Lord Did Not Pray.*

The Pulpit and the Well of Life

ON THE BACK OF THE PULPIT of the Church of the Open Door, in downtown Los Angeles, is placed the well-known scriptural injunction, "Sir, we would see Jesus." This familiar Scripture is found in many pulpits today as a constant and urgent reminder to the preacher of the primary purpose of the pulpit.

After mentioning to the Board of the Church that I had seen this Scripture in so many pulpits, they placed it on the pulpit of the Church of the Open Door without any suggestion on my part. This direct imperative is appropriate in an age that has witnessed the reduction of the pulpit to a soap box for the propagation of a philosophical nostrum, a side-show barker's platform for any religious racket, and the stage for the entertainment of habitues of church buildings.

There is an added motto which might be placed helpfully alongside the scriptural injunction. It is not scriptural but is very familiar to our contemporary society. The motto is, "This Is Your Life."

The pulpit is a mirror held up to the life of the minister, and the life of the minister flows—all unconsciously to him— through the pulpit. Diligent study habits will be reflected from the pulpit; laziness and carelessness become obvious in the glare and searching spotlight of the pulpit. What is in the "well" of his life will come up through the "bucket" of the pulpit. This frightful fact was given to me as a student in seminary, and the experiences of a quarter of a century have corroborated the accuracy of this thesis.

The contemporary pulpit is immeasurably weak. This is not a day of great preachers. The present-day preacher is an organizer, a promoter, a counselor, a youth director, a Christian Education expert, a builder, a money raiser, and a "good fellow" in the community. He does not need to be a man of God and a great preacher of the Word of God, according to modern standards.

In spite of warped and perverted attitudes toward the preacher and the pulpit, there are three objectives that I have attempted to keep in mind in the preparation and delivery of a sermon.

SIMPLICITY IN PREPARATION

There is a pernicious and contagious disease which has recently affected the ministry which can be designated as "neo-intellectualism." There is a definite aim to make the sermon a masterpiece of erudition. The attempt seems to be to take simple truths and make them complex rather than take profound truths and make them simple.

It was said of our Lord Jesus Christ, "And the common people heard him gladly." Even Paul, the intellectual giant, wrote to the Corinthians who boasted of their worldly wisdom: "And I, brethren, when I came to you, came not with excellency of speech or of wisdom, declaring unto you the testimony of God. For I determined not to know anything among you save Jesus Christ, and him crucified" (I Cor. 2: 1, 2).

It was fortunate for me that during my college days I met a very scholarly minister who had the knack of taking the profound truths of theology and translating them into the simple language of the ordinary person. I asked him for his secret. He assured me that this priceless gift was one that needed to be developed and cultivated. His formula went something like this: In the preparation of the sermon every effort should be made to attain simplicity—then go over the sermon the second time to reduce it to the simplest common denominator. Go over the sermon again and again until you are ashamed of its simplicity, then preach the sermon so that the children can understand it. Afterward, one of the spiritual saints will come up to remark about the depth and profundity of the message. It is difficult to make the message too simple.

The preachers of the past and present who have ministered to the crowds spoke in the language of the common people. The late Dr. Harry A. Ironside, who spoke to thousands each week of his ministry, had two homely expressions which are apropos:

> Jesus told us to feed His sheep, not His giraffes.
> Put the cookies on the bottom shelf for the kiddies to get.

This method is fully illustrated in the Bible relating to the reading of the Law by Ezra on a pulpit of wood before the Water Gate:

> ·So they read in the book in the law of God distinctly, and gave the sense, and caused them to understand the reading (Neh. 8:8).

SCRIPTURAL IN CONTENT

The old-fashioned methods of preaching were topical, textual, and expository. There is a tendency today to depart from all three—in fact, to depart from Scripture altogether. Sermons have become "pep talks" on psychology, political speeches on the United Nations, or propaganda for some new fad. Someone has defined the modern church as a place where a mild-mannered man gets up before some mild-mannered people and urges them to be more mild mannered.

The expository sermon is not passé, it is still the only effective method of reaching the hearts of the listeners. An entire passage should be considered in a sermon. The passage should be read and studied until it is mastered, then it should be arranged in a logical division. The sermon should be more than a running commentary on the verses. Painstaking study will reveal a logical division and method of presentation in every passage.

The preacher who uses the Word of God has the Holy Spirit to lead him and to apply the Word to the hearts of his listeners. A preacher who departs from Scripture in. his preaching robs himself of his greatest assistance. The Word of God is still "the sword of the Spirit." Likewise, the Holy Spirit will give him added insight: "But as it is written, Eye hath not seen, nor ear heard, neither have entered into the heart of man, the things which God hath prepared for them that love him. But God hath revealed them unto us by his Spirit: for the Spirit searcheth all things, yea, the deep things of God" (I Cor. 2:9, 10).

Furthermore, God has promised to bless His Word and

not the pet theories of the preacher: "So shall my word be that goeth forth out of my mouth: it shall not return unto me void, but it shall accomplish that which I please, and it shall prosper in the thing whereto I sent it" (Isa. 55:11).

Sermon content is far more important than preparation and delivery. The man who is filled with the Word of God will find a way of giving it forth: "And if I say, I will not make mention of him, nor speak any more in his name, then there is in my heart as it were a burning fire shut up in my bones, and I am weary with forbearing, and I cannot contain" (Jer. 20:9, A.S.V.).

Sincerity of Expression

There is a grave danger of the preacher becoming professional in the pulpit. He can easily become an actor who is merely playing a part. The theoretical and academic are to be studiously avoided. He should not major in that which he has not himself experienced. Spiritual life and the deeper things can only lead to pride if the preacher has not grappled with them in his own experience. Certain doctrines may become an obsession rather than the practice of the preacher. The head so easily runs faster than the heart.

Unfortunately, there are men in the ministry who are sincere but their voice ministers against them. There are others who have a sincere voice but are engaged in a religious racket. This is especially true of the radio. Spiritually-minded Christians will eventually make the distinction. All of this should not preclude the minister from being sincere in his own ministry.

Three messages must be prepared a week by the average preacher; and preach, he must, whether he likes it or not. Therefore, he should seek, in prayer before God, a burning heart. He should speak as Wesley said: "A dying man to dying men!" McCheyne wrote, "Speak for eternity." Paul stated it in the language of the Spirit: "Woe unto me if I preach not the gospel." The prophet cried that the Word was a fire shut up in his bones.

The preacher who does not love to preach should carefully examine his call to the ministry. It should be the burden of his soul. The Lord Jesus Christ could report to the Father, "I have given them thy word!" I trust that this statement can be put in your final report and in mine.

The Human Story

Genesis 3

J. VERNON McGEE

THERE IS A QUESTION which every thinking mind has asked. You have asked it. It has even invaded the field of nursery rhyme as found in "Where's an Answer?"

> Where did you come from, baby dear?
> Out of the everywhere into the here.

"Whence came man?" has been the common question down the ages, and it demands an answer. The statement of reply given in this little rhyme is neither scripturally nor biologically accurate, but it faces the problem of origin.

Where did the human race begin—what is the origin of man? Many explanations have been offered. Some have been popular for awhile and then discarded as lacking evidence. When I was a boy sixteen years of age I read Darwin's *Origin of Species* and then his *Origin of Man*. But Darwinian evolution is discredited today. Dr. Arnold Brass made a tremendously revealing statement in his little pamphlet concerning Dr. Haeckel, an evolutionist. He said that Dr. Haeckel published forgeries in his book to prove his theory. Dr. Haeckel in replying said, "I should feel utterly condemned and humiliated by the admission [he did admit that he had done just that] were it not that hundreds of the best observers and most reputable biologists lie under the same charge. The great majority of all morphological, anatomical, historical, and embryological diagrams are not true to nature, but are more or less doctored, systematized, and reconstructed." And it was Dr. Watson, the great English evolutionist, who made the statement, "Evolution is a theory universally accepted, not because it could be proven to be true, but because the only alternative—special creation—was clearly incredible."

One of the reasons, I suppose, for the acceptance of evolution by so many is that it offers an "out" for man, and he does not have to accept the Biblical account of creation. Without evolution man today is on the horns of a dilemma and has no theory. One agnostic recently declared, "We do not have to offer an explanation for the origin of man." In spite of his statement, man's mind cries out and wants a reply to the question, "Whence came man?"

For more than three thousand years Scripture has presented a record of the origin of man. At first it had to overcome the superstition and idolatry of bygone days, and today it withstands the speculation of this scientific age. It is couched in noble terms; it is written in lofty language. The latest findings, when laid in parallel by the Genesis account, give cause for singing the "Hallelujah Chorus." How majestic Genesis reads in our day!

As important as man is in our thinking, the Bible does not open with the story of his creation, it opens with the fact of God. He is the One who is pre-eminent in this Book. Should the whole world turn to atheism it would not alter the fact that there is a God and that He created all things.

We are told that God created the heavens and the earth first. One summer I had the privilege of listening to Mr. Chestnut, a wonderful Christian layman who heads up the Department of Research of the General Electric Company. He told us that it has been demonstrated in the laboratory that matter can be created out of energy. This is a more difficult process than that of breaking down the atom, but it has been accomplished. Having told us this, Mr. Chestnut then burned into our minds a passage from God's Word when he quoted: "By faith we understand that the worlds were framed by the word of God so that things that are made were not made out of things which do appear." In other words, energy and power have been translated into matter. The Word of God is "quick and powerful." God spoke and energy was translated into matter. This fact we have understood by faith. Today it is demonstrated in the laboratory.

Let us get another thing clear in our thinking. Genesis was not written as a scientific statement. Does that startle you? I thank God that it was not, and here is my reason for that statement: It will compare with present-day scientific statements, but science is a changing subject, and if Genesis were written in the science of the hour it would be wrong twenty years from today. The Nebular Hypothesis of La Place was good science years ago, but it is now discarded. Man changes his theories as he progresses in searching. No, the Genesis record is a religious record, and we should learn to compare it with the cosmogonies of that day.

Does it contain scientific error? A few years ago we were told that it would not stand, for it mentions light on the first day and does not mention the sun, moon, or stars until the fourth day and that light cannot be had without light holders. But Genesis was accurate in those days of scientific attack, for we now know that there was light before there were light holders, for cosmic light is a light that needs no light holder. So the Genesis account stands!

After Genesis 1:1 a great catastrophe occurred . . . earth became without form and void. A curtain went down on the pre-Adamic creation—an iron curtain. There was, and is, no penetration of that curtain and anything that man says is pure speculation. You can put behind that curtain all the ages you may care to for this earth, but never forget that you are dealing with a God of eternity, and this little earth on which we live has been here a long time. Perhaps millions, billions, or terms of years known only in the language of eternity.

We have here in Genesis six days of renovation, preparatory to a new tenant arriving. Now man is created and we are vitally concerned with him. This little earth becomes the center of interest in this universe so far as the Bible record is concerned. Formerly it was uranicentric—pertaining to the heavens; then the record changes to the geocentric—pertaining to the earth as the center. The telescope has been laid aside and now the microscope comes to use. No longer is it the study of the macrocosm—the universe, but the microcosm—man, human nature.

Here is the record that is given: "These are the generations of the heavens and of the earth when they were created the day that the Lord God made the earth and the heavens." Each time I read the Scriptures I find something new. It has been embarrassing for me to find something new in the first chapter, but I did that this time. We read: "These are the generations of the heavens and the earth." Notice carefully—the heavens are mentioned first. Then when He begins to talk about man it reads: "In the day when the Lord God made the earth and the heavens"—there is a rightabout face; the earth becomes the center of interest because man is to be created and put on this earth.

Just here we want to note a word, the use of which is peculiar to Genesis. It is the word *generations,* and every time it is used it always gives the generations that are to follow, and the generations of the heavens and the earth are the generations of man. Now notice something that is quite wonderful, and in looking at it keep in mind the fact that when He speaks of the generations of the earth He is not speaking of what has preceded, but what follows; He speaks of results and not causes; it is a superscription, not a subscription, and the creation of man follows. Will you notice it: "The Lord God formed man and breathed into his nostrils the breath of life and man became a living soul." Man is at once the offspring of Heaven and of earth. This is the generations of the heavens and the earth, and now God takes dust—man is of the earth earthy—but God breathes into his nostrils the breath of life. Man is not only of the earth, but man is of Heaven. In fact, three stages are given here of creation:

> I. Genesis 1:1—The first creation—matter
> II. Genesis 1:21—The creation of life—whales, etc.
> III. Genesis 1:27—The creation of man—with a spiritual world.

These three phases find their conclusion in Paul's great statement: "That your whole body, your soul, and your spirit might be preserved unto the coming of Jesus Christ."

On the physical plane man is kin to the animal world; he is made of the same kind of dust. Now just because a Ford automobile has four wheels, two headlights, and one steering wheel does not mean that it was made in the same factory as a Chevrolet. They are different though they both have four wheels, a steering wheel, etc. They are made this way because they are both going to operate on the same place, the highway. Man has two eyes, he has two ears, and he has a mouth; certainly he does for he is physical, and so does the animal world. But this does not prove anything. It merely proves that on the physical side he was made of dust, which the Scripture says. On the psychological side he has a soul, the functional part of man with drives and urges. Then there is his spiritual side which came from God when God breathed into him the spirit of life. Man has a humble and a high origin. He is both earthy and heavenly. God created, out of dust, one in His own image, and we are told that He remembers we are dust. The psalmist said, "I am fearfully and wonderfully made."

Man the creature was made a free moral agent. He was given the right of choice between good and evil, which is essential to personality. Having been given this right of choice he was put under test, not one involving crime, but that of obedience to God. Here we find that the Devil tempted man who, instead of resisting him, listened. Man doubted God, denied the commandment of God, and disobeyed. Disaster came and man became depraved.

Genesis 3 is the most important chapter in the Bible in explaining the tragic fruits of disobedience from the Garden of Eden through the centuries of man's march to the present hour. This chapter draws a clear picture of the life of the city in which you live. In Genesis 1 and 2, you see man created and placed in the Garden of Eden. Now read chapter 3 which delineates our modern life, and you cannot but conclude that man is not in the Garden. Something tragic has happened—man disobeyed God. If you want to know how great was that disobedience and how tragic the results, listen to the apostle Paul as he looked at the human story, and said: "Because that when they knew God they glorified him not as God, neither were thankful, but became vain in their imaginations and their foolish hearts were darkened, professing themselves to be wise they became fools and changed the glory of the uncorruptible God into an image made like unto corruptible man, and birds, and four-footed beasts and creeping things; wherefore God also gave them up to uncleanness." If you will look around you in your city today, you will see that uncleanness in countless thousands of lives.

As the result of man's sin a fourfold judgment fell. First of all, there was a judgment upon the serpent. The Lord said unto the serpent: "Because thou hast done this thou art cursed above all cattle and above every beast of the field; upon thy belly shalt thou go and dust shalt thou eat all the days of thy life." Upon the animal world about us is this judgment of God. Paul writing of it in Romans 8 says: "For the earnest expectation of the creature waiteth for the manifestation of the sons of God; for the creature was made subject to vanity, not willingly."

Now while there is this judgment resting upon the serpent, beyond the serpent there was one, Satan, and we read that there was a judgment to come upon him: "The great dragon was cast out, the old serpent, called the devil, and Satan, which deceiveth the whole world, who was cast out into the earth and his angels were cast out with him."

And still another judgment was pronounced, and it was upon woman. God said that in sorrow now she is to bring forth children, but He also said: "I will put enmity between thee [the serpent] and the woman, and between thy seed and her seed; it shall bruise thy head, and thou shalt bruise his heel." Beloved, go to Bethlehem—that is God's work here, not man's—"Behold a virgin shall bring forth a child." Go to Golgotha; that is God's work, not man's—it is dark and the night will come when no man can work. There was a transaction between God the Father and God the Son when He bore the penalty for the sins of the whole world. Yes, judgment came upon woman, and upon this earth, and today the whole creation is travailing in pain, waiting for a deliverance that is coming through the redemption that is in Christ.

Then we find that a fourth judgment came, and it was upon man. Listen as God speaks to man: "In the sweat of thy face shalt thou eat bread, till thou return unto the ground; for out of it wast thou taken: for dust thou art, and unto dust shalt thou return." Whether we consider man with a crude implement of the Stone Age or see him surrounded with the gadgets of this push-button civilization, it is still true that it is by the sweat of the face that he eats bread.

This, then, is the human story. It is a sad story—the sob

of the city, and the sigh of the countryside. We find life filled with irritations, annoyances, disappointments, and resentments. Men's hearts are filled with frustrations, tensions, complexes which often lead to some high bridge or building and a dash to death. It is a story of broken homes, hungry children, and neglected old people. The lullaby of Broadway is a theme in which the drunkard, the harlot, and the thief weave their way into the stream of honest folk. The light of Liberty is gone out. Bitterness and wrath are in the hearts of men; envy and hatred are among nations, and strife and gossip are in the house of God. Scripture says: "Men shall be lovers of their own selves, covetous, boasters, proud, blasphemers, disobedient to parents, unthankful, unholy, without natural affection, truce breakers, false accusers, incontinent, fierce, despisers of those that are good, traitors, heady, high-minded, lovers of pleasures more than lovers of God; having a form of godliness, but denying the power thereof" (II Tim. 3:2-5).

But that, thank God, is not the final chapter. It is true that "by one man sin entered the world, and death by sin," but also that as "by the offense of one judgment came upon all men to condemnation; even so by the righteousness of one the free gift came upon all men unto justification of life" (Rom. 5:18).

Today there stands a cross between us and the Garden of Eden; that cross is not an ambulance sent to a wreck! He is the Lamb of God slain before the foundation of the world. The cross is not God's second best, it is His very best. Genesis 3 closed with the record that the cherubim were put there to keep the way of life. They were not to block it. God said: "In spite of man's sin I will keep the way of life open for him." And we see in Revelation 5 a company of every tribe and nation of the earth standing before Him saying: "We have been redeemed unto God by thy blood, out of every tongue, tribe and nation over the earth."

Now listen, guilt came upon man, but today "who shall lay anything to the charge of God's elect?" Today God justifies. "Who is he that condemneth?" "There is therefore now no condemnation to them which are in Christ Jesus" because Jesus died, He arose from the dead, and today is at the right hand of God "where he ever liveth to make intercession for us," and "who shall separate us from the love of God?" Back in the Garden of Eden man was separated. Paul gives us comfort and security when he says: "I am persuaded, that neither death, nor life, nor angels, nor principalities, nor powers, nor things present, nor things to come, nor height, nor depth, nor any other creature, shall be able to separate us from the love of God, which is in Christ Jesus our Lord."

Today we have gained more in Christ than we lost in Adam, and I would rather be in the midst of this perverse civilization with Christ than in the Garden of Eden without Him. In Christ we have hope, salvation, deliverance, and security.

Back in the Garden of Eden God said to man: "In the sweat of thy face shalt thou eat bread" (Gen. 3:19, A.S.V.). But today, because He sweat great drops of blood, as it were: "We can take, eat of his body which was broken for us."

HAROLD JOHN OCKENGA

Born in Chicago, Illinois.

A.B., Taylor University, 1927, D.D., 1937; L.H.D., Suffolk University, 1939; Hum.D., Bob Jones University, 1944; L.C.D., Houghton College, 1946; Th.B., Westminster Seminary, Philadelphia, 1930; A.M., University of Pittsburgh, 1934, Ph.D., 1939.

Assistant minister, First Presbyterian Church, Pittsburgh, 1930-1931; minister, Point Breeze Church, Pittsburgh 1931-1936; Park Street Church, Boston, 1936—; president, Fuller Theological Seminary, Pasadena, California, 1947-1954; president, National Association of Evangelicals, 1942-1944; Conference Speaker and World Missionary Traveler.

Author: *These Religious Affections; Our Protestant Heritage; Every One That Believeth; The Comfort of God; The Spirit of the Living God; The Church in God;* and others.

A Hard Lesson to Learn

THE SERMON IS A MESSAGE FROM GOD, not an essay, or treatise, or Bible reading. It should be born in prayer, or devotion, or Bible study, or in the fire of human experience. This was one of the hardest lessons for me to learn. Some ministers never learn it. Let me illustrate.

I did my first preaching in an evangelistic team of four men, who traveled about as invited. One member of the team was older and more experienced in preaching than the others. After I had preached a few times, he came to me and said, "Ockenga, what you preach is not a message. It is a Bible reading." I did not understand him, but all summer long he kept repeating this thought in different ways. It actually irritated me. Toward the close of our tour I had a deeper Christian experience which shook me to my foundation spiritually and which caused me to search the Bible concerning the Holy Spirit. After I passed through a personal appropriation of the Pentecostal work of the Spirit, I prepared a sermon expressing the truth I had learned. After I preached it for the first time, my friend came to me and said, "Ockenga, that's the first *message* I have ever heard you give. Now you can preach!" I knew what he meant and ever since I have never been satisfied in preaching unless I have had a message from God. This assurance of a divine message is essential to effective preaching.

Where does the preacher get his message, so that he literally is a man sent from God? There are many ways to originate a message. The first is Bible study. Following this experience I began to practice several kinds of Bible study. One consisted of concentrating on a particular book, by reading and rereading it, and then writing everything which came to me on each text individually. When a complete thought had been treated, I organized my ideas about it into a logical outline, with a theme and title. By spending one half-hour a day in this exercise I covered the Book of Matthew in two years, and discovered that I had about one hundred sermon outlines. Many of these I have never used, but the practice developed a method and kept me amply supplied with Biblical topics and texts. Later I learned that this is called inductive Bible study, but I had arrived at it by personal discovery.

It should be said that no commentaries or supporting books were used in this Bible study. The Bible communicated itself and its message. This practice in my early ministry gave me my expository method.

While reading in Reformation history I learned that Ulrich Zwingli, while at Einsiedeln, Switzerland, began at the first verse of Matthew and preached through the New Testament. When he was transferred to Zurich he simply continued this method. The net result was that he preached himself out of the Roman Catholic system and into the Reformation. Zwingli lived contemporaneously with Luther and was totally independent of Luther as a Reformer. Upon learning this, I determined to use the same method. For five and one-half years of my Pittsburgh ministry I preached through book after book of the New Testament—John's Gospel, Acts, Romans, I and II Corinthians, Galatians—all on Sunday mornings. Truly, since this was my first major effort on this line, it was limited. But I was trying my wings to reach the proper stride or level of my gifts. By the time I began my ministry in Park Street in 1936, I was primarily an expository preacher. Hence, I began at Matthew 1:1 and in twenty-one years have preached through the entire New Testament at my Sunday morning and Friday evening meetings.

The advantages of expository preaching are many. One is that the preacher is never left groping for subjects or topics. His study of the Word keeps unfolding topic after topic in an endless stream. Another is that by this means every subject of life is sooner or later treated, without being dragged in. When the Bible speaks of tithing, the preacher does. When the text deals with adultery or fornication, the preacher does. When the context touches upon human government, or politics, or economics, or education, the preacher takes the principles and develops them in a modern setting. Thus the whole counsel of God is given to the congregation. Another advantage is the indoctrination of the congregation in the great Biblical truths, principles, and experiences. People and preacher are educated in Biblical theology simultaneously. Let me illustrate.

On one occasion I was to be absent from my pulpit for three weeks. Several of my intimate ministerial friends had recommended a certain preacher to supply at Park Street. I had never heard the man but since I needed a supply and could trust the judgment of these friends, I invited him to occupy my pulpit during my absence. He accepted, but after he preached his first sermon some complaints were made to the board of deacons concerning his loyalty to the Bible. After his second week in the pulpit the people in general requested the board of deacons to cancel the remainder of his engagement. The deacons refused.

The point is that the people had become so indoctrinated by expository preaching that they immediately recognized where this preacher was not true to the Bible, even when fellow preachers did not. This was the only such experience of this nature we have had in twenty-one years, for our people are tolerant of much, but not of preaching disloyal to the Bible.

Bible study by the preacher will originate many messages from the inspiration of truths impressed upon him such as redemptive love and sacrifice, humility, loyalty, service, etc. Again he will be impressed by the biographies of Biblical characters, a most prolific source of sermons on human attributes, temptations, tribulations, and triumphs. The Bible is faithful in narrating the sins and failures of the heroes of the faith, but never to condone them. A biographical sermon or series of sermons never fails to evoke interest and to provide the framework for the finest kind of preaching. I use these on Sunday evening and have preached on every major character of the Bible, plus many minor ones. Sunday evening is the time for doctrinal preaching also. Christians appreciate intelligent, careful, up-to-date treatment of the major doctrines of the faith. My last series of twenty-one doctrines drew many students and filled the church every Sunday evening. Once or twice a year I give a short series of four or five sermons on prophecy. The times are such that the headlines of the newspapers carry Biblical names and refer to

Biblical places, so that one almost thinks he is reading his Bible. People want to know the meaning of these events, and the preacher has a great opportunity to utilize these to proclaim the authority of the Word, to explain God's revelation, and to apply the spiritual admonitions and exhortations connected with the fulfillment of prophecy. Care must be exercised at this point not to ride a hobby, or to set dates, or to foist an arbitrary system upon the Bible, or to make a system of prophetic interpretation a test of orthodoxy. I also find that current events provide topics for timely presentation of Biblical truths. The preacher must be alert to utilize the channels of popular thought for the inculcation of God's message.

I never hesitate to interrupt an expository series, or doctrinal, or biographical, or prophetic series to use an occasional sermon topic for Christmas, Thanksgiving, Easter, Pentecost, or any other day of the church calendar. More and more, Christians are expecting sermons appropriate to the calendar of the church year and are disappointed when they do not receive them. I do not hesitate to redeem the opportunity of daily preaching in Lent or Holy Week. Great truths may thus be communicated to sensitive minds and hearts. In our own church year we have established set seasons for a missionary conference, a Christian education conference, an evangelistic campaign, etc. This gives ample opportunity for intensive emphasis upon these subjects and for resultant commitment and participation on the part of the congregation. In addition, awareness of human needs gained from pastoral calling, personal counseling, and public catastrophes may be used to present special truths and to urge spiritual experiences, so that the preacher has a wealth of sources from which his sermons may originate.

The second step is to outline the subject. Once the topic and theme are impressed by God on the preacher's heart so that he has a message, he should proceed to develop his outline. Next to his theme the outline is the most important step in the preparation of the sermon. The outline must express the original idea. Let it be fresh, new, individual, personal. Do not use another man's outline. Make your own. I spend more time on this step than on any other. Since I preach without notes, I find the outline is the key to my effectiveness. The outline must express what is the text, context, or topic. It must be logical, so as to carry itself. Here the use of the syllogism is invaluable. The completion of one major point must naturally and automatically leave the preacher before his next point, so that his memory is not taxed too greatly. Only logic will do this. Any system of memoronics such as alliteration, parallelism, or contrasts will help. Some definite form should be developed which is natural and easy for the individual. Then that form of sermon structure should be followed. I generally have an introduction, three major points, and a conclusion, with three subpoints under each section, all in alliteration. All this is part of the outline and is designed to keep me from forgetting and to impress the message on the hearer. Let me illustrate.

A friend preached a very unusual and impressive Mother's Day sermon on Proverbs 31, dealing with a virtuous woman. I was thinking about it a few days later. The sermon had four points. I could remember three—the first, second, and last—but I could not remember the third even though I knew the verses on which it was based. At a reception that same week I asked for a review of points. He did that but said he could not remember the third point. The others were Industry, Fidelity, and Sympathy, but neither of us could remember the third. A few days later he saw me and said, "Now I remember. It was personal interest." I said, "Why didn't you give it a title like courtesy or generosity to make a parallelism so we could remember it?" He replied, "Oh, I didn't have time for that. It was coincidental that the others were parallel." I pointed out to him that this was the reason neither he, the preacher, nor I, the hearer, could remember the third point in the passage of Scripture. No man can preach without notes unless he observes these rules concerning his outline. Put time into it, for it will repay you. In addition, outline your conclusion first, so that you always keep in mind your goal, your aim, your purpose, and then you will not be shooting at random.

The third step is the obtaining of material for the sermon. Some people place this second or even first but that is a mistake for it ruins originality or spoils logical development. When the topic and theme are chosen, and the outline logically forged, then is the time to gather material for the flesh on the bones. Reading in the original languages or version should be done in connection with the outline, but if it hasn't it must be done now. The nuances of meaning of the Biblical text must be mastered and often throw much light and provide much material. The related texts and passages of Scripture bearing on the subject must be examined and used here. Next the student should examine his file for general material, illustrations, and library references for material throwing light upon his topic and theme. Finally, let him refer to commentaries, critical and practical, to ascertain whether he has missed anything important by way of emphasis or teaching. The content of the sermon depends upon the thoroughness of this third step. Often I never get to the commentaries at all, for I have a complete message without them. I am much happier when this is the case.

The fourth step is to reoutline the message in the light of the material gathered. The process pertains only to the subheads of your own outline. If the original work was done well the resulting will be very minor. But it is wise to reexamine the outline in the light of all available facts and information.

The fifth step is to write out or to dictate the sermon. For the first fifteen years of my ministry I wrote or dictated every sermon. This develops a preacher's style. The vocabulary, phraseology, sentence structure, figures of speech, etc., come from work in writing. Once this is established firmly the preacher may abandon the practice. Now my sermons are all recorded on tape and disc, but often I dictate a message for printing. The ease with which this is done is the result of fifteen years of early labor in forming a method, a style, and a facility. Thus I dictate all the books I write at this stage. It is easier for me to dictate than to write, for my thoughts flow faster than I can write them.

The sixth step in preparation is to memorize the outline. I have to prepare and deliver three major sermons and two minor addresses in Park Street Church every week, besides all outside speaking engagements. Thus I prepare my Sunday evening sermon first. Next, I prepare my Friday night exposition. Finally, I prepare my Sunday morning sermon. Thus it is easier for delivery. I deliver the Friday night lecture while it is fresh in my mind. Then I work on Saturday on the Sunday morning sermon, finishing it and getting it in mind to deliver. On Sunday afternoon I revert to the evening sermon which was prepared first in the week, getting it in mind to preach without notes. In this way I unload my mind in the reverse order of preparation and avoid confusion. It takes me about two hours to memorize my outline. While I do this memory work, I bathe my heart and mind in prayer. The ease of one's memory work will depend upon the care with which he made his outline.

The seventh and last step is to preach the sermon. Leave manuscript, notes, and material on your desk when you enter the pulpit. Enter with a trust that God will bring all things to your mind which you knew. What He wants you to forget let go by. What He wants to amplify, He can do by the power of suggestion. Thus you have liberty in preaching, direct address to the people, and give sway to the work of the Holy Spirit. This has been my method for thirty years of preaching without notes and no doubt will be as long as God allows me the great privilege of expounding the unsearchable riches of Christ.

Dr. Luke Testifies of Physical Resurrection

Harold John Ockenga

*Behold my hands and my feet, that it is I myself;
handle me, and see; for a spirit hath not flesh and bones,
as ye see me have* (Luke 24:39).

NUMEROUS ARE THE EASTER QUESTIONS and affirmations. One question is, Did Jesus of Nazareth survive the crucifixion in some spiritual form of continuity of life? Almost every line of thought except materialism and naturalism admits that He did, but such an affirmation is not necessarily Christian. It may simply be synonymous with a survival of influence, or of spirit, or of ideas. There are many nebulous thoughts of the continuity of life expressed at Easter time, thoughts which are beautiful but not necessarily Christian.

Another question is, Did Jesus of Nazareth, who was crucified outside of Jerusalem in A.D. 29 or 30, rise again from the dead? Was His body so reactivated that it came forth from the tomb? This is an entirely different question from the former one and the writers who are delightfully clear on the fact of Jesus' death by crucifixion are tragically vague when it comes to handling this subject. They seem to be enveloped in an agnostic fog at this crucial point, quite in contrast with the New Testament Scriptures and with the Christian creed. The Christian faith unqualifiedly declares that Jesus of Nazareth did come forth from the tomb in the same body in which He had been crucified, and it bases its faith to a large extent upon the testimony of the beloved physician, Luke, who believed in the physical resurrection of Jesus. In the joint work, Luke-Acts, this physician stated the evidence which is the ground of the New Testament faith in the resurrection.

Another Easter question is, Do Christians believe that they as believers will have a physical resurrection? This again is quite a different question from faith in Christ's resurrection. Will the body in which we live, suffer, and die, rise again? To put it very practically, let me use an illustration. On Patriot's Day the mayor of Boston, accompanied by many notables, a band, a contingent from the Army and from the Navy, marched into the Granary Burying Ground next door to Park Street Church to conduct a service in memory of the patriots of Massachusetts. With flags flying and soldiers standing at attention, taps was played, prayer was offered, a short speech was given in memory of John Hancock, Samuel Adams, James Otis, and Paul Revere whose bones lie moldering in those graves. Do we believe that these patriots will come forth from the tombs and graves in the bodies in which they lived their tumultuous and interesting lives?

Some who believe that Christ arose physically from the dead cannot believe that Christians will have a physical resurrection, yet Dr. Luke believed this and the resurrection of Christians is an article of Christian faith. Hence, we say in the Apostles' Creed, "I believe in the resurrection of the body." It is the physical resurrection of Jesus which enables us to believe in the resurrection of the body of the believer.

I. Dr. Luke's Experience Authorizing Him To Speak

Let us look at this man Luke. He was a doctor. He was called by Paul in his Colossian letter "the beloved physician." He had probably studied medicine in the university of Tarsus and had taken the oath of Hippocrates. Luke was a scientist. He used the scientific method, or the processes of induction, whereby he learned by experience. There are many people in this congregation like him today. Do you want to use the inductive method of discovery, of arriving at the generalization from the observation of the particulars? Well, that is the way a scientist ought to be and that was the way Luke looked at things.

Luke came into contact with Paul at Antioch. In one of the early manuscripts of the Book of Acts the word *we* is appended to 11:28, suggesting that Luke was present at the Antiochian ministry of Paul and Barnabas. It is apparent from the New Testament that Paul suffered some kind of malady. We are not sure what his sickness was. It probably was something pertaining to his eyes. On the Damascus Road Paul had looked into a blinding light, above the lightness of the sun, and was blind for three days. Later, he tells the Galatians how they would have plucked out their eyes for him if they could, he refers to writing his letters in a large hand and he often used amanuenses, and he tells us that he prayed three times for the removal of his thorn in the flesh. God did not answer Paul's prayer affirmatively but promised that His strength would be made perfect in weakness and that His grace would be sufficient for him. It is thought by most Bible students that Paul suffered some kind of eye disease.

On the first missionary journey we have no reference to Luke; but when the second missionary journey begins we find him dropping into the first person in the narration of the trip from Troas to Philippi, revealing that he was with Paul at that time. An examination of the Book of Acts reveals these "we" sections bring Luke into companionship with Paul on the second missionary journey, and again on the third missionary journey, traveling with him from Philippi to Jerusalem, and then that Luke was with him on the shipwreck journey from Caesarea to Rome. The time of

Luke's conversion is not stated but if he came from Antioch as is supposed, then he was converted out of a Libertine society, which was devoted to the worship of the goddess Daphne and which was noted for its licentiousness and its easy way of living. Probably Luke was caught up in the revival movement at Antioch where the disciples were first called Christians. When the Holy Spirit said to the Antiochian church, "Separate me Barnabas and Saul unto the work whereunto I have called them," Luke watched the commissioning service. He probably even envied John Mark his opportunity of going with Paul and with Barnabas on that first missionary journey. When John Mark turned back, returning to Jersualem from Paphos, Luke was critical of him as is revealed in the tenor of his narrative. Then, when Paul and Silas started on the second missionary journey, Luke joined the party and cast his lot with the apostle and his cause.

From that time on Luke's ministry is identified with the ministry of Paul with whom he was a companion. He speaks about the Lord "calling us to preach" in Macedonia. He felt that the mission to Macedonia was given to him. He identifies himself with Paul and Silas in the struggles at Philippi. He undoubtedly attended Paul after his beating and imprisonment. Luke must have remained at Philippi, for he was silent about the rest of the second missionary journey and the early part of the third journey; but when Paul reaches Philippi on the third journey, Luke again drops into the first person in the narration of the story, revealing that he resumed his travels with Paul. Luke was Paul's amanuensis in the writing of some of his letters. He also was an excellent storyteller and as he traveled about the Mediterranean with Paul he gathered materials for the Gospel which he was later to write and which was to be an official history of the Christian religion, proving it to be a licit religion so as to avert persecution. We may presume that Paul's ideas are freely reflected in Luke's writings, just as Peter's ideas are reflected in Mark's writings. Therefore, what Luke thought about the resurrection was an echo of the convictions of Paul. Hence, we find a close correspondence of fact between the epistles of Paul referring to the resurrection (cf. I Cor. 15) and Luke's narration of the event of the resurrection, both in his Gospel and in Acts.

When Luke took it in hand to write his Gospel, it was to draw up an account of the "things most surely believed" to his friend Theophilus who needed instruction in the truth and who may have subsidized Luke's writing. The Gospel by Luke is an historical treatise giving a chronological treatment of the Gospel from the birth to the ascension of Jesus according to the best information which was available from the eyewitnesses and the sources. Luke established the certainty of his facts from written sources extant at that time, from traditions, and from the testimony of eyewitnesses and ministers of the Word. His travels gave him an unusual opportunity to interview the eyewitnesses of the miracles, of the crucifixion, and of the resurrection itself. The convictions of Luke as a physician as well as the fruit of his historical investigations as a scientist are reflected in the Gospel and in the Acts. Luke was a painstaking historian.

II. Dr. Luke's Evidence Concerning Physical Resurrection

This evidence is very interesting to me and I think it will be to you. When you open the Gospel according to Luke, what do you find? First, you find a unique emphasis upon the birth narratives of Jesus Christ. There is the story of John the Baptist, with the annunciation of Gabriel to Zacharias, with the preparation of Elisabeth, with the nature of the child to be born, and with a delineation of the ministry he was to perform. Following this comes the announcement made by the Angel Gabriel to Mary at Nazareth concerning the virgin birth, the nature of the Child to be born, the position He should hold over the kingdom of David, and the fact that He should be conceived by the overshadowing of the Holy Ghost. Luke records the reaction of Mary at this announcement and her submission to the angelic command. In the hymns of the Magnificat and the Benedictus, and then the actual narration of the birth of the Lord Jesus Christ, attested by the worship of angels, Luke lays great emphasis upon the physical body of the Lord Jesus.

Nevertheless, we should note that whether it was in the annunciation of the angel, in the testimony of Elisabeth to Mary, or the Benedictus of Zacharias, or in the testimony of John the Baptist to Jesus, or even in the announcement of the angels at the birth of Christ, Luke consistently and repeatedly bears witness to the supernatural; namely, that this Child who was born was both God and man, that He was pre-existent but that He took upon Himself a real body by a virgin birth. Hence, in the emphasis of Luke we have a true incarnation with a permanent union of two natures in one Person. Dr. Luke laid the basis for the Chalcedonian Creed concerning the Person of our Lord Jesus Christ.

When you as a reader come to the conclusion of the Gospel of Luke, you find him greatly interested in the crucifixion, in the death of Jesus, in His being taken down from the cross, in His being wrapped in a shroud, in His being laid in a tomb, and in the sealing of that tomb by the Roman authorities after the soldiers had given evidence of His death. Luke's attention is centered on the body. He even draws emphasis to the fact that Mary Magdalene, Salome, and Mary of Cleopas attended the body as it was laid in the tomb. Luke refers to the body of Jesus seven times as if to call attention to it: five times as it was laid in the tomb and twice as being absent from the tomb at the time of the resurrection. He wants to make it clear that it was the body which was put in the tomb which also came out from the tomb.

A careful reader of Luke's Gospel will note that the thing which interested the doctor on the resurrection morning was that the physical body of Jesus was gone from the tomb. His record is a lovely, beautiful, and enchanting story (24:1-12). He tells of the women as they came to the tomb with their spices to anoint the body on the first day of the week, he relates their shock when they found the stone rolled away and the sepulcher open, he relates their consternation in finding that the body was gone and their anxiety to report this to the apostles. How anyone can say that Luke had no interest in the body in the light of his narrative is hard to understand.

The next thing Luke narrates is the story of the living Christ. He tells of the appearance of two angels, "men in shining garments," reflecting the light of Heaven, who brought fear upon and reverence from the women. The announcement made was, "He is not here, but is risen." This is the positive proclamation of the Easter fact in addition to the negative evidence of the open tomb. Said the angel, "Why seek ye the living among the dead?" From that day forward their interest was in the living Christ. The living Saviour was identified with the body which they sought. The angel said, "He is not here." This body of Jesus was the first fruits of the physical resurrection. Said the angel, "He is risen." It is perfectly proper to respect the bodies of our loved ones, to lay them away reverentially in a tomb or a grave, to place flowers in their memory, for we are attached to those bodies and as Christians we believe that they will rise again. The angels reminded them that this was according to their Lord's word. Many times He had prophesied to them that He was put to death, would be buried, and would rise again on the third day; but the disciples were unable to believe this until the events fulfilled His prophecy.

Luke then reports how the women informed the eleven disciples. In response, Peter and John ran to the tomb. No more accurate depiction of this is found than England Burnand's picture of these two disciples going to the sepulcher. Anxiety and expectation are depicted on their faces, their garments are swept by the wind as they run toward the sepulcher to see if the report of the women is true. Seeing the reality of the empty tomb, Peter wondered within himself at that which was come to pass. Truly, the empty tomb, the absence of the body, and the reported resurrection were wonderful.

The next bit of evidence Dr. Luke advances concerning the physical resurrection is the attestation of it in the appearances of the living Christ. Here we confine our remarks to those appearances narrated only by Luke in chapter 24. First, the two disciples were on their way to Emmaus (24:13-35). One was Cleopas, the husband of Mary, mother of James and Joses, and an intimate follower of our Lord Jesus Christ. As these two disciples were walking to Emmaus and talking about the events which had happened at Jerusalem, including the report of the women that the tomb was empty, a Stranger joined them and asked: "What manner of communications are these that ye have and are sad?" They responded: "Art thou only a stranger in Jerusalem, and hast not known the things which are come to pass there in these days?" He said unto them, "What things?" and they told him about Jesus of Nazareth, a mighty prophet who had done great deeds, whom the chief priests and rulers had condemned to death and had crucified. Then they betrayed their lack of faith in declaring that they had hoped that it should have been He who would have redeemed Israel. Following this, the stranger began at Moses and the prophets and showed unto them that Christ ought to have suffered these things and to have entered into His glory in accordance with the Scripture. Before they knew it they were at Emmaus and they pressed Him to receive their hospitality. While He was breaking bread with them, they recognized Him and He disappeared from them. With hearts still burning with a joy which an understanding of the Word concerning the events which had occurred created in them, they rushed back to Jerusalem with the testimony that they had seen the Lord. Luke here emphasizes that Jesus walked, talked, and ate with two disciples over a period of at least two hours, thus giving evidence of the physical nature of the resurrection.

The next emphasis of Luke is upon the appearance to Peter. Wherever or whatever this appearance was, we do not know, but we do know that Peter was convinced that he had seen the Lord. What happened that day from dawn at the sepulcher and dark in the upper room for Peter is a matter which we will have to ask him when we get to Heaven: but somewhere, during that day, the Lord appeared to Peter.

The next emphasis of Luke upon the resurrection is of the Lord's appearance in the upper room (24:36-48). First He assuaged their fear by asking them why they were troubled and pronouncing peace upon them. Next, He assured them of His identity, saying, "It is I." In support of this, He asked them for meat and they gave Him a piece of broiled fish and some honeycomb which He took and ate before them. Next, He applied the Old Testament Scriptures to His death and resurrection, opening their understanding concerning the law, the psalms and the prophets. Finally, He announced the nature of their work in the proclamation of the fruit of His death and resurrection in the forgiveness of sin. In the midst of all this the emphasis is upon the properties of the body. Luke speaks of "hands and feet," of "flesh and bones." Jesus says, "Handle me and see . . . it is I." He says, "Have ye any meat?" Luke declares that Jesus "ate before them." What greater attestation could one want of a physical identity and existence than this? The fact that the Lord Jesus Christ came and went, appeared and disappeared, merely attests that it was a resurrection body with new powers in addition to the old.

The final evidence of the resurrection of Jesus' body was

given by Luke in the record of the ascension. Luke tells us that He tarried with them for forty days, speaking of the things pertaining to the kingdom of God. He appeared to them again and again. He taught them many things. He ate with them. He walked with them. He invited them to handle Him. Finally, He took them out on the familiar road to Bethany, and without any further word except the extending of both of His hands toward them in blessing, He was taken up from them and disappeared in the Shekinah of glory. Luke is definite in the translation of the God-man in a body from earth to Heaven, and then relates the announcement of the angels that He will come again in that same body. On investigation, Luke's writings reveal that there can be no reasonable doubt that Dr. Luke recorded the Christian belief in the physical resurrection of Jesus of Nazareth.

III. Dr. Luke's Emphasis upon the Scriptural Framework of the Resurrection

Not only did Dr. Luke emphasize the physical resurrection of the Lord Jesus Christ, but he did it in a Biblical framework. In all these narrations concerning the appearances of the resurrected Christ, Luke shows how that this was in accordance with the Scriptures. On the Emmaus road the emphasis is, "Ought not Christ to have suffered these things, and to enter into his glory?" Then, opening the Scriptures pertaining to Himself, Christ showed them from Moses and the prophets the overwhelming evidence of the necessity of His death and resurrection which caused their hearts to burn within them. In the upper room He also opened the law, the psalms, and the prophets (cf. Pss. 16; 22; 110; Dan. 7:13), showing the necessity of His death and resurrection. After the event of the opening of their understanding, it was easy for the disciples to see the application of the Scripture. How we today can fail to understand this is difficult to see! If our Lord so emphasized His resurrection in a Biblical framework, and if Luke and the disciples so understood it, how much more should we place the truth of the resurrection in the New Testament framework of the completed revelation which we have today.

In Luke's story of the history of the apostolic Church contained in Acts, he gives a prominent place to the resurrection. This was the apologetic doctrine of the apostles wherever they preached for the sake of conversion. Peter made it his main doctrine at Pentecost. There he used Psalm 16 and Psalm 110 which he declared were fulfilled in the resurrection of Jesus Christ and in the coming of the Holy Spirit. He also used the resurrection as his main doctrine when he preached at Solomon's porch (Acts 3:12-18). Again, when Peter stood before the Sanhedrin, his emphasis was upon the resurrection (Acts 4:11; Ps. 118:22). An illustration of Paul's missionary preaching is given in Acts 13, describing his sermon at Antioch, in Pisidia. There also, he quoted from Psalm 2 and Psalm 16, declaring that they were fulfilled in the resurrection of Jesus Christ from the dead, through whom men could have the forgiveness of sin. All of the apostolic preaching emphasized the cross as the means of atonement and the resurrection as the seal of God upon this redemptive work for the salvation of men. This is the doctrine Peter preached to the household of Cornelius (Acts 10:40 ff.) and which Paul preached at Athens (Acts 17:31 ff.). Dr. Luke thus applied the truth of the resurrection in the framework of Biblical doctrine. He declared that God raised up Jesus in attestation that all will be raised up and brought into judgment. The fact that Jesus was raised from the dead proves that there will be an assembly of all men in the judgment of God (Acts 17:31). Luke's travel companion, Paul, expounded the great truth of the physical resurrection of Christ as the evidence of the resurrection of the believer. If Christ arose from the dead, He was the first fruits and we will be the full fruit. We shall have a body like unto Christ's (cf.

I Cor. 15). The argument is that Christ arose, therefore we shall arise; Christ had a resurrection body, our body will be like unto His: powerful, immortal, incorruptible, and spiritual; Christ is coming again, we shall be made like Him in a moment when He comes: the change will take place in the twinkling of an eye. Thus, Luke lays the groundwork for a Gospel of full salvation for all men; not only a continuity of the spirit of man after death, but a resurrection of his body. Redemption is not complete until the glorious, triumphant redemption of our bodies.

Heaven, therefore, is not a nebulous place of shadows, or a limbo of spirits, or a condition of common life in which we are lost in the infinite as the drop of water returns to the ocean, but it is a place of individuality, of personality, of physical completion and of intercommunion. We believers will have access to and mastery of this magnificent universe in bodies which are redeemed and made like unto the body of our Lord Jesus Christ. Today our universe is measured in billions of light years, and stars are numbered in galaxies in which each galaxy has a billion individual stars and where there are billions of galaxies. There is a day coming when God will have transformed this world and our own bodies into the likeness of the Lord Jesus Christ, when at the speed of thought we shall have access to and mastery over this universe which God has created. Let there be no teaching of a dark limbo for me. I will take the scriptural teaching of a continuity of personality, a resurrection of the body, and individual identity in a glorious redeemed universe in which we will be the heirs of God and the joint-heirs with Jesus Christ. Jesus said, "Because I live, ye shall live also." This is the Easter message. Hence, Jesus said: "Behold my hands and my feet, that it is I myself; handle me, and see; for a spirit hath not flesh and bones." We shall be like Him. Our whole personalities will be redeemed through the efficacy of the cross and the resurrection.

ALAN REDPATH

Born in Newcastle-on-Tyne, England.

Durham University School; Wycliffe Hall, Oxford.

Chartered accountant; six years as executive with Imperial Industries, Ltd., the largest industrial combine in Britain.

Itinerant evangelism for four years with Christian Youth Movement; for thirteen years pastor Duke Street Baptist Church, Richmond, Surrey; pastor, The Moody Memorial Church, Chicago, Illinois, 1953—; city-wide evangelistic campaigns in a number of the largest cities in Britain; "Faith for the Times" campaign, Royal Albert Hall, London, 1944; "Festival of Britain" campaign, London, 1951; "Deeper Life Conventions" at Keswick and elsewhere; three speaking tours to America and Canada.

Author: *Victorious Living, Victorious Praying;* and *Victorious Christian Service.*

Five Principles of Sermon Preparation

THERE ARE THREE ELEMENTS in any sermon: first, the form of it which involves the study of homiletics; second, the substance of it which involves a study of the Word of God; and third, the power of it which comes through the holiness of the preacher and through constant waiting upon God. Any man, who boasts that half an hour before he preaches he has no idea what he is about to say, may be sure that half an hour afterward nobody will know a word that he has said. It is far better to pray and never to preach than preach and never to pray.

The ultimate object of any sermon is to gain the assent of

the will of the congregation. This objective may be approached along the line of the emotion and the intellect, but it must lead to the intake of the will. In other words, the preacher is concerned about securing a verdict. There are certain principles, therefore, in every message which have to be observed:

The Germinal and Terminal Law. By the first of these I mean that we must get the theme and the essential content of the message from the Word of God and by the inspiration of the Holy Spirit. Only so can preaching be with the power of God. By the Terminal Law I mean that the objective of the message must be kept in view all the time. If the text controls the preacher, he may give good exposition. If a theme controls him, he will deliver a fine essay; but if the object controls him, he will be preaching a sermon. Therefore, first of all, we must be sure of our objective. If you start with the subject, you may well accommodate the text to the theme rather than the reverse. In such cases, the germ is in the preacher's brain rather than in the mind of God. Again if you start with a text which seemed attractive and make an exposition of it, you may by ingenuity interest and instruct the congregation but fail to grapple with the conscience and the will. Power in preaching results from a clear objective in view which burdens the heart of the preacher.

The Law of Impression and Expression. Truth must impress itself on the heart of the preacher before it can express itself on the congregation. You cannot separate the man from the message. The power of expression depends upon the depth of impression. Truth must be held and embedded in the mind of the preacher until it takes root. We have to chase our wandering thoughts because we are powerless to grip other people unless the truth has first of all gripped us.

The Law of Inclusion and Exclusion. A sermon must include the whole man. He must have placed in his message his whole heart and must be in his preaching and every facet of his personality given over to the delivery of the Word of God. The Law of Exclusion will mean that he must shut out all unfair dealing with truth and every hindrance to the work of the Holy Spirit. If truth would be transparent and living to the hearts of the people, he himself must be transparent before God.

The Law of Flow and Glow. (Or if you prefer it—The Law of Flurry and Fervency.)   Fullness of matter and ample preparation must be secured in order to insure freedom of utterance. Flow, that is fluency in delivery, depends upon ample material. The preacher should always have more available than he can use, and he will hold something in reserve. He will have much more material behind him than he brings to the front. This can only come by disciplined meditation upon the Word of God. The Law of Glow, that is to say the fervency, the reality with which the preacher gives utterance to the message, depends upon the experimental application of the text to his own life. Truth must lay hold upon the preacher and mature in his own life or else he will soon be preaching beyond his experience and without the Holy Spirit's power.

The Law of the Fundamental and Ornamental. By this I mean that the basis of the sermon must claim our attention first. Ornamental features must be subordinate to this. The foundation must be broad, firm, scriptural, and spiritual. Any illustrative matter is only justifiable in so far as it is clearly applicable to the fundamental message. I find it most helpful to write out a message in full before preaching it. Then in actual delivery avoid the use of notes as far as possible.

So much for some of the principles I seek to observe in the ministry of the Word of God. Perhaps I should add that it is my conviction that the message, which lives and burns as a fire in the heart of the preacher, is that which he has received from the Lord Himself in his own personal quiet time and waiting upon God. Commentaries and other textbooks may be useful additions, but this surely is the supreme thing in all ministry. We are not intended to be copies of other people in the truth we present, but rather to be original. God has an individual pattern of ministry for every one of us. For that reason I find that a "Seed-Thought Book" is a most valuable part of the equipment of my personal devotional life. As the Word of God speaks in a quiet time, I register in the book some verse or promise which has stood out and then leave it there, remembering that our devotional life is not the time for the preparation of sermons but rather the time for feeding our own hearts. To return to the "Seed-Thought Book" for further study and to work at the text as the carpenter works among the shavings on his bench is to find the material beginning to burn and take fire in one's heart. Complete dependence upon the Holy Spirit is essential in every aspect of ministry. For it is "not by might nor by power, but by my Spirit, saith the Lord."

The Art of Winning a Soul for Jesus

ALAN REDPATH

PERHAPS TO MANY OF YOU, this subject of witnessing and soul-winning brings almost a blush to your face in the recognition that you have never really seriously attempted to lead anyone to know Jesus Christ as his Saviour. To others it brings a sense of shame because so often they have failed. Perhaps there was a time when you began to speak a word, but maybe from the derision of the one to whom you were speaking or the laughter or the jesting of others, or the opposition which you faced, you somehow were quickly silenced.

Others perhaps are conscious that they have sought to witness for Christ but their witness has been so ineffective that people, instead of being drawn to the Lord, have been driven away. This subject is a very vital one for each one of us. It is the key to blessing in the whole Christian life.

In Acts 8:26-40, there is a classic example from the life and lips of a man called Philip. Philip was not one of the apostles. He was a deacon. Strange to say that the Gospel first reached the uttermost parts of the earth, not through an apostle, but through a deacon. Philip apparently had soon left the serving of tables to preach the Word. He had been commissioned to this task and was the first one to announce the good tidings to the great continent of Africa. There are many precious lessons that we may draw from this example of soul-winning. It is something that concerns every one of us because the principles are the same whether God desires us to be witnesses in Africa or whether He desires us to be witnesses here at home. No soul is won for Christ without someone having paid a price, without travail, without sacrifice, and here is an example of it. Here are some principles of witness in Philip's life.

I. He Was in a Position To Hear the Voice of God

"The angel of the Lord spake unto Philip" (v. 26). Philip was in a position to listen to God's voice. That may seem a very insignificant thing to say, but I consider it supremely important. Philip was a busy man; he was the leader of a great movement of revival, he was living under extreme pressure. He was constantly being sought out for counsel, and for advice. There was the excitement of the movement of God's Spirit, there were hundreds of people being converted, and he was literally living in the whirl of all this, amid the tremendous pressure of the work of God. A significant uprising of the Spirit had occurred in Samaria. He had preached Christ in that city, and there had been a mighty turning to God through his ministry. This man, living in all the excitement of blessing, living amid all the thrill of seeing a work of God, was yet in a position to hear God's voice. Philip in the midst of life under pressure never lost the spiritual tone, never lost the sense of the nearness of the Lord Jesus, never lost the consciousness of his walk with God. He was not too busy. He listened to the voice of God.

Are you in a position today to hear God's voice? It is so easy in the business of Christian work to lose the reality of the Word of God; so easy in the pressure of it all to become desperately barren; so easy to be so busily occupied in study, in books, in theories, in administration, in service, that if God speaks we would be too busy to hear, and what God has to say we would lose. Philip in the midst of pressure preserved spiritual tone. He listened to God's voice.

II. HE OBEYED GOD'S COMMAND

"The angel of the Lord spake unto him, saying, Arise, and go toward the south unto the way that goeth down from Jerusalem unto Gaza, which is desert. And he arose and went." That is all! Do you see the significance of that tremendous obedience? It is expressed here so simply. To Philip, Samaria was the place of fellowship, the place of Christian friends, the place where loved ones assembled, the place where perhaps he often received help and counsel from others. In addition, he was the very center and leader of it. Surely this man was indispensable in such a situation, when suddenly the voice of God spoke to him and said: "Philip, go down to the way that leads toward the south which is desert." Here is the leader of a revival being sent away from preaching to a crowd, away from a multitude, away from the context of all the surroundings to which he had been accustomed and all the Lord said was: "Go in that direction and all I am going to tell you about it is that it is desert." Philip had nothing to fear. He had learned a secret in his life, and it is the only secret that will keep a man in such a situation living victoriously—instant obedience.

It was the angel of the Lord who spoke to him in Samaria, and when he went into the desert and met one man, it was the Spirit of the Lord who spoke with him and told him to link himself with the chariot. Philip was independent of crowds because he was dependent upon the Holy Ghost. He had so grown and so preserved his spiritual integrity that he knew that he need fear nothing, even in a desert. Because God sent him there, God would go with him. The same Spirit who had spoken in the pressure of Samaria, spoke to him tenderly in the loneliness of the desert. He obeyed God's command.

III. HE HURRIED AFTER ONE UNSAVED SOUL

"Philip ran thither to him, and heard him read the prophet Isaiah and said, Understandest thou what thou readest?" (v. 30). If God gives you the privilege of ministering to a crowd, ask Him to deliver you from losing your love for the individual soul; ask Him to save you from becoming professional; ask Him to save you from becoming used to it; ask Him to save you from being careless or indifferent to the needs of one person.

The Ethiopian eunuch is a tremendous character who flits across this page, as it were, in God's Word. He is come and gone in a chapter and we do not hear of him again. Here was the first person to whom the Gospel was preached in the uttermost parts of the earth, and he was a Negro. He was the chancellor of the exchequer in Ethiopia; he was over all the queen's treasure; he was under her supreme authority; he had command of all her riches and all her wealth.

Three hundred years before Christ, history tells us, a very cultured civilization had built itself up in that part of Africa. Greek culture had reached that country. Certainly there was no question on his part of being illiterate. He could read and as he read, he began to wonder. As he wondered he began to sense hunger in his heart and a desire in his soul. He read in the Book about Jerusalem and decided to make a 1,200-mile journey across a desert to reach it. I can picture the chancellor of the exchequer with his servants and with his retinue moving away from the queen's courts for this long journey. He was a key to the continent of Africa. Unquestionably he was a man of great authority and intellect and education, but all these things fall aside as I think of him as a man with a hungry heart, a longing soul—dissatisfied. He had been to Jerusalem to the temple, to the place of worship, and he was more mystified than ever on his return trip. He had found no light, no understanding; and he was sitting in his chariot reading the prophecy of Isaiah. Here was an Ethiopian who traveled 1,200 miles to learn the truth and was going back from the place where he thought he would receive light, still completely in the dark. Suddenly a messenger from Heaven spoke to a Christian and said, "Go and attach yourself to that chariot, and Philip *ran*." He hurried after one unsaved soul.

IV. HE USED THE WORD OF GOD IN SOUL-WINNING

"Philip opened his mouth at the same scripture and preached unto him, Jesus" (v. 35). What scripture? The Ethiopian had been searching and had come to Isaiah 53. As he read it aloud with a mind that was utterly in the dark and a heart that longed to have understanding, Philip came to him and said, "Understandest thou what thou readest?" "How can I," he said, "except some man guide me?" Philip had one theme in his soul-winning, he preached from the same scripture—Jesus.

This lovely disciple, this unobtrusive character had one passion in his heart, it was to preach Christ and to preach a full Jesus, and from this precious portion of the Word he sat down with the Book open and preached the One "who was wounded for our transgressions and bruised for our iniquities." As Philip preached Christ, that man's heart was melted, and the tears began to fall down his face as he understood for the first time, and his hungry soul was satisfied. He knew now the truth which had been hidden from him. For the first time in his life, there came into his heart the peace of God that passes understanding.

V. PHILIP LED THIS CONVERT TO THE NEXT STEP

"He commanded the chariot to stand still; and they went down both into the water, both Philip and the eunuch; and he baptized him" (v. 38). Here was a man going back into a pagan, heathen, dark country, the only Christian in the whole continent, and before he went back he was burning his bridges behind him. He was making a public confession of his faith in Christ. Philip was not content to leave him until there and then, out in the open before his whole company of servants and soldiers, he had made his stand for the Lord Jesus and confessed Him in the waters of baptism. Philip was doing the job thoroughly.

VI. HE LEFT THE CONVERT TO THE CARE OF THE HOLY SPIRIT
(perhaps the greatest of all the arts in soul-winning)

"When they were come up out of the water, the Spirit of the Lord caught away Philip, that the eunuch saw him no more: and he went on his way rejoicing" (v. 39). Rejoicing? What had that man to rejoice about, going back to a continent where he would meet no other Christians, going back to face ridicule and persecution? But he went on his way rejoicing!

We have no reference here to the coming of the Holy Spirit on him, we have no reference here about tongues or the laying on of hands. Here is another indication of the sovereign working of the Spirit of God. This man went away rejoicing. Just in the same way that Philip had faced a desert, this new convert would face a continent in the name of Christ. He went back rejoicing. Philip had faith to believe that the work was done and that the Spirit of God would care for this young child in the faith.

Centuries before this incident the psalmist said: "Ethiopia shall haste to stretch out her hand to God." From the throne in Heaven one day the Lord Jesus—ascended, risen, triumphant—saw the chancellor of the exchequer of Ethiopia becoming conscious of his ignorance and of his need, and the Spirit of God began to work in the life of this man who could revolutionize the whole country by his influence. God saw this man in an isolated, heathen land with nobody to help him, nobody to point him to Jesus. God looked down upon another country and saw a man in Samaria, called Philip, a man living in close touch with his God, and took hold of Philip and sent him to the desert. At the same moment, God had timed it so that the Ethiopian eunuch would make that journey, and the two met. That Negro heart, filled with longing and unhappiness, was satisfied.

Suppose Philip had not gone and suppose that he had not obeyed! Millions of people like this Ethiopian chancellor are stretching out their hands to God for light, and how shall they hear if they have no preacher? They are to be found on the Amazon, South America, Europe, China, Russia, Philippines, Malaya, Far East, all over the world, and in Chicago. Men and women with hearts that are dissatisfied, hungry, empty—and God sees them.

Does it matter—one man with an empty heart and no disciple? In the sovereign plan of God, His whole plan of redemption is frustrated for that individual, and God holds us responsible for the man's eternity. "If the wicked shall not hear, his blood shall be upon thy head."

Are you prepared to obey God's command and stir yourself from your nest of comfort and seek a soul for Christ?

PAUL STROMBERG REES

Born in Providence, Rhode Island.

A.B., University of Southern California; D.D., 1923; Asbury College, D.D., 1944; Houghton College, L.H.D., 1953.

Associate pastor, Pilgrim Tabernacle, Pasadena, California, 1920-1923; ministerial superintendent, Detroit Holiness Tabernacle, 1928-1932; pastor, First Covenant Church, Minneapolis, 1938-1958; president, National Association of Evangelicals, 1952-1954.

Special speaker and Bible teacher in Billy Graham Crusades in London, Scotland, and New York; radio and conference speaker.

Author: *If God Be For Us; Things Unshakable; The Radiant Cross; Stir up the Gift; Christian Commit Yourself; Skyways of the Soul;* and numerous pamphlets.

A Sermon Is Born

A N ANALOGY FROM NATURE is only roughly helpful, for I find that the gestation period of a sermon varies from instance to instance. Even that statement is subject to correction, because in point of fact the origin of one's sermon, like most origins, is lost in mystery.

Let me therefore assume that general preparation for preaching is taking place all the time: in wide reading, perceptive observation, reflective thinking, interacting conversations, disciplined Bible study, communion with the Holy Spirit.

With me the "impregnation" that is eventually to produce

a sermon takes place when text and topic are set down on a
3″ x 5″ card and put away. From time to time memoranda
are added: an outline, perhaps, or an illustrative suggestion,
or reference material.

It is time now, let us say, to decide what will be the sermon
for a particular service; or to vary the putting of the matter,
to determine what I feel to be the guidance of the Spirit of
God for this or that hour of preaching. In fresh commitment
to the Holy Spirit I go over these cards. To be sure, I bring
to this quest some more or less specific concern: the knowledge, for example, that the sermon will be preached on Easter
morning, or the beginning of Universal Prayer Week, or
the closing Sunday of the Missionary Conference; or quite
differently, with some urgent awareness of a problem or need
on which I feel the full resources of the Gospel should be
brought freshly to bear in the life of the congregation.

If this sensitive searching of the homiletical incubator fails
to find anything warm enough for "delivery," I must give
myself to further prayer and reflection—until a text and its
linked theme really "come alive" within me.

Normally the procedural matters that follow are these:

A fresh examining of the context. This may involve a
rereading of a whole book. It must involve a careful re-
examination of the relevant passage from which the text is to
be taken. Here I try not to forget G. Campbell Morgan's
lean dictum: "A text without context is a pretext!"

*A reading (often half-aloud) of the text in several differ-
ent versions of the Bible.*

Enlisting the aid of the exegetes and expositors. If there
is a knotty problem in interpretation that is involved, I may
consult as many as ten or a dozen "authorities."

The building of the outline. If this has gone at least as
far as the "main heads" at some time in the past, all the better. It is now time to give it careful scrutiny to see if it stands
up to one's present thinking and desires. If it doesn't, then it

must be worked over or discarded in favor of something more suitable. In any case, it is my habit to scribble the fuller outline on a piece of paper, evolving the subheads gradually until something of wholeness and balance has been achieved.

The searching of files. The central theme will, of course, suggest certain subjects on which one has been filing away material for years. Similarly, the several aspects of truth that the sermon will attempt to illuminate suggest subjects on which resource-data have been accumulated. How delicious the moment when one finds in the file a nugget of a quotation, or a statistic, or an illustration that fits the need as neatly as a kid glove fits a hand!

Consulting other preachers who have published sermons on the text or, at any rate, the subject that one has chosen. Manifestly, this is not for the purpose of imitating them but rather of catching inspiration from them. I have met a few ministers who say they never read other men's sermons. I find it impossible to share their feeling. Currently I have between seven and eight hundred volumes of sermons in my library. My incurable interest in expository preaching leads me, understandably enough, to the works of men who are saturated with the Word of God and endowed with the ability to expound it.

The writing. One of the two Sunday sermons (in my case the one given in the morning at which time the service is broadcast) is normally written out fully. The evening sermon is written out in copious notes, and sometimes as fully as that of the morning. I wish I could report that the preparation of the week was out of the way by Saturday afternoon. My admiration tends to rise in a salute to the preachers who are able thus to manage their work-week. If defense is needed, I suppose it could be pointed out that my ministry frequently takes me away from home and the parish between Sundays. Hence the toil and sweat of preparation (which I can honestly say is almost never drudgery but, contrariwise, sheer delight) will, for me, go on deep into the Saturday hours and will consume my Sunday afternoons as well.

Using the manuscript. While I neither read nor memorize the sermon, I do try thoroughly to absorb what has been prayerfully written. The manuscript is before me as I preach, but it is there chiefly as an aid to accuracy in the use of statistics or quotations. It is my unshakable conviction that preaching must be living *encounter* between preacher and listener. Anything is either harmful or irrelevant that keeps the Word of God from *getting through,* from establishing vividly this "I-thou" relationship.

Giving attention to introductions and conclusions. It is a conviction that grows with the years that the first few sentences of a sermon are of priceless importance. They should somehow seize the minds of the listeners, giving to them the feeling, "Ah, this is going to be worth my hearing!" Perhaps the fact that our Sunday morning service has been on the radio for the past eighteen years has made me more than ordinarily conscious of the penalty a speaker pays for an introduction that loses rather than gains attention. *How* and *when* to conclude are likewise considerations of such vital urgency that I have wrestled with them in an honest attempt to combine passion with common sense. I dread giving people the impression that when the time has come to leave Interpreter's house I am as a man wandering about, confusedly looking for an exit.

Preparing the preacher. Approximately twenty-five hours out of each week are spent on what might be called the direct and intensive preparation of the two Sunday sermons. In all of this there is one indefinable factor, never easy (for me at least) to disengage from the preparation of the *sermon,* and that is the preparation of the *preacher.* The two are interlaced and interlocked. Of this I am unalterably convinced: unless the soul of the preacher is in tune, the sermon will be out of tune.

The Drama of the Double Search

PAUL STROMBERG REES

"Where art thou?"—Genesis 3:9
"Where is he?"—Matthew 2:2

HERE WE HAVE THE FIRST of God's questions in the Old Testament and the first of man's questions in the New.

In what circumstances did they arise and what do they suggest?

We come upon the first question in the Genesis account of the wrong turn that man took very early in his history. The theologians call it the "fall." John Milton, the poet, calls it "the first disobedience."

In the loneliness, in the sense of lostness, that came to guilty Adam he heard the voice of God calling to him. As its accents rose and fell, it seemed to him that all he could hear was, "Adam, where art thou?" The seeking God, in holy judgment but in patient love, was on his trail. Adam could not pile so high the shattered fragments of the old fellowship but that God would climb over them to find him.

That is the setting of the first query.

What of the second one?

RESTLESS LIGHT

The city is Jerusalem. The time is nineteen hundred years behind us. The visitors—the Magi—have come a long way. If there was a light above their heads, there was a light

149

also in their eyes—the eager, restless light of hope and long-ing. The world needed a deliverer. Israel needed a Messiah. They had somehow heard the prophetic Word. The haunt-ings of destiny were in their souls. Hence their arrival in Judah's Holy City and their fervent query, now to one per-son and now to another, "Where is he that is born King of the Jews?"

"Where art thou?" God asks it, looking for man.

"Where is He?" man asks it, looking for God.

It's the drama of the double search, and it's infinitely im-portant.

There are several things I want to say about it.

I. Two Quests—and Both Are Urgently Real

That's the first thing.

For God, life is *unsatisfied* without man; for man, life is *unbearable* without God. The whole Biblical story of man's creation, downfall, and renewal is mightily revealing as to the kind of God who acts to save men in the stormy field of this world's life.

A. *"I'll make Me a man!"*

You must start by picturing the kind of God who created man. We read of Jesus that He "ordained twelve, that they should be with him" (Mark 3:14). He wanted their com-panionship. Perhaps that's a clue to the motive behind the creation of man. God made us because He wanted our com-panionship.

Is not that what caught the imagination of James Weldon Johnson when he wrote those rather startling lines called "The Creation"?

> And God stepped out on space,
> And He looked around and said:
> "I'm lonely—I'll make Me a world."

So the physical creation came into being—sun, moon, and stars, mountains, seas, and animals. But God looked around on all He had made and said, "I'm lonely still; I'll make Me a man!"

And the poet goes on:

> This great God,
> Like a mammy bending over her baby
> Kneeled down in the dust
> Toiling over a lump of clay
> Till He shaped it in His own image;
> Then into it He blew the breath of life,
> And man became a living soul.

But the loneliness of God soon returned. For that "living soul" He made chose death—the death of disobedience, and self-worship, and alienation from the Creator.

So began the divine quest for the recovery of that lost fellowship. This in fact, is what the Bible is all about. It is the meaning of what we say when we use the word *salvation*.

And if you think the Wise Men who trekked from Persia to Israel to find the Christ Child made a long journey, consider the distance God had to travel to find the heart of alien, rebel man.

B. *Wide is the gap*

How far is it from white to black? How great is the distance from holiness to sin? What is the mileage from humility to pride? How wide is the gap between God-centeredness and self-centeredness? Here are measurings that you can't register on the mileage mechanism of your speedometer. Here are calculations that are more than geographical.

Still, whatever the distance, God traveled it—bit by bit, stage by stage. First He sought out men in whose hearts He could plant His dreams—an Enoch here, and an Abraham there, and a Moses yonder.

Then He found a people—a chosen, covenant people—with whom He would enter into solemn relations and through whom He would make a witness to all nations. When men everywhere were given over to the worship of idols, and corrupted thereby, it was a very great thing for one branch of the Semitic peoples—Israel—to hear the message: "Hear, O Israel: the Lord our God is one Lord; and thou shalt love the Lord thy God with all thine heart, and with all thy soul, and with all thy might" (Deut. 6:4, 5).

But then, strangely enough, God kept reminding Israel that a greater revelation of Himself was ahead of them. Within this community of the covenant prophets would arise, saying, "Keep your eyes on God." He will yet do a greater thing! Thus they heard their Isaiah say: "Unto us a child is born, unto us a son is given: and the government shall be upon his shoulder: and his name shall be called Wonderful, Counsellor, The mighty God, The everlasting Father, The Prince of Peace" (Isa. 9:6).

C. *The seeking God*

And so it came to pass! The seeking God, no longer content with priests and prophets, came Himself! And later, when the Holy Child had become the Holy Man, He made it clear as day that the seeking God had never altered His quest: "The Son of man is come to seek!" "The Son of man is come to seek and to save that which was lost" (Luke 19:10).

Know this, dear man, whoever you are or however far you seem to be from God, He seeks you. He longs for you. He is lonely without you.

But then, the other side of this matter is crucially urgent too: you are lonely without Him. You may or may not admit it, but you are.

And something deep within you—deeper indeed than all of your denials of it, or your forgetting of it—cries out for Him: "Where is He?" Every lost man, whether skid-row shuffler or boulevard stepper, has a God-shaped blank at the heart of him. It's an emptiness that God alone can fill.

If you want it expressed in the language of the scholar, listen to Prof. Hocking, of Harvard: "Man comes up to a certain point and then he finds he hasn't resources in himself to complete himself, so he remains incomplete and frustrated." The cry is there, you see: "Where is He?"

D. *Inner poverty*

If you want it in the language of everyday, earthy experience, here it is in the conversation of a wealthy New Yorker and his wife who, after making a fortune and losing their souls in the big city, were visiting the little town where they grew up. With a nod at the town, the husband remarked, "Well, that's where we came from, dear." Her reply released a hidden ache: "Yes, and I'm just wondering where we got to!" The outer plenty was no answer to the inner poverty. The deep-down quest was not dead: "Where is He?"

Certainly! For it's almost impossible to kill it.

II. Two Quests—and Each of Them Ends in a Costly Surrender

Take the first: "Where art thou?" How costly was it to God to pursue that quest?

The great message of the Old Testament is: God beckons to man. The great message of the New Testament is: God becomes man.

John puts it in language that is simple and stately: "And the Word was made flesh, and dwelt among us" (John 1:14). But listen to Paul's description of God's coming in Christ: He "stripped Himself of all privilege." (See Phil. 2:6-8, Phillips for entire passage.)

That's costly surrender! So costly it's hard to picture. Just the same, let's try.

A. *Fit for a King*

Let your mind fancy a man who is far and away the richest and the handsomest you ever saw. He lives in a palace. He has been educated by the most brilliant tutors. He eats, from the most immaculate linen and tableware, foods that are fit for a king. He is surrounded by the appropriate evidences of his vast wealth—imported furnishings, rare works of art, books by the most famous authors bound in the finest covers, music that is produced by the masters, and cultured companions to sharpen his wits and make gay his days.

Now imagine a young woman who lives down a dingy street in a foul slum. She is without beauty, without charm, without learning, without funds. Her awkward and untidy feet walk on carpetless floors. The walls that stare at her from morning to night are soiled and bare. Her food is the poorest. Her clothes are worn and tattered. Her features are ugly and repugnant. You might sketch her with Kipling's awful line: "a rag, and a bone, and a hank of hair."

Your imagination isn't equal to the next step, but strain at it anyhow. Picture that wealthy prince of a man making his way to that hovel of a place and setting his heart on that woman. To win her, he moves from his mansion to a tenement next door. He will prove to her that this suit of his is not an act. He means it. At the level of her squalor and dinginess he lives, till the day arrives when he says. "Mary, I love you. And if you will give me your love, I'll take you away with me, and life will begin all over again."

Well, that is a faint picture—feeble and faulty indeed—of the costly surrender God made when, seeking wretched, unhappy, foolish, warring, stricken man, He came to Bethlehem and to Calvary.

"Where art thou? O man, where art thou? I love you. I want you."

That's God side of the search! Costly beyond words!

But there's the other side: *ours!*

B. *Quivering lips*

Look now at those Wise Men, on whose quivering lips are the words of our second question: "Where is He?" Their quest also ended in a costly surrender. For we read: "And when they were come into the house, they saw the young child with Mary his mother, and fell down, and worshiped him: and when they had opened their treasures, they presented unto him gifts; gold, and frankincense and myrrh" (Matt. 2:11).

I am not excited over speculations, however sensible or fanciful, as to what those three substances represent. I am concerned only with the plain fact that they surrendered to Christ the costliest treasures they had.

And surrender is still the price of finding Him. Here, for example, is a young man, accompanied by his fiancée, coming to a minister to talk over the proposed marriage. Although she is a professing Christian, he is frank to tell the preacher that he has no interest in God or the church. The pastor, tactfully but firmly, points out that successful marriage must have a spiritual foundation, that where there is not mutual understanding about such basic matters as the Christian faith there is serious reason to doubt how happy or permanent the marriage will be. Would the young man surrender his prejudices and consider honestly the claims of God upon his life? He would. So the preacher sent him away with two books to read, both of them by authors who know how to get down to brass tacks in this business of helping people into a saving experience of God.

A month later, which was one week before the wedding, the minister asked him how he was getting along. The young man said that he had surrendered enough to start praying. "But," said he, "where does Jesus Christ come into all this?"

"One Solitary Life"

The pastor lifted from his desk a card, on one side of which was a picture of Christ and on the other side the striking thumb-nail biography of Jesus called "One Solitary Life." Handing it to the young man, he said, "Read this:

> Here is a Man who was born in an obscure village, the Child of a peasant woman. He grew up in another obscure village. He worked in a carpenter shop until He was thirty, and then for three years He was an itinerant Preacher. He never wrote a book. He never held an office. He never owned a home. He never had a family. He never went to college. He never put His foot inside a big city. He never traveled two hundred miles from the place where He was born. He never did one of the things that usually accompany greatness. He had no credentials but Himself. He had nothing to do with this world except the naked power of His divine manhood. While still a young Man, the tide of popular opinion turned against Him. He was turned over to His enemies. He went through the mockery of a trial. He was nailed to a cross between two thieves. His executioners gambled for the only piece of property He had on earth while He was dying—and that was His coat. When He was dead He was taken down and laid in a borrowed grave through the pity of a friend.
>
> Nineteen wide centuries have come and gone, and today He is the Centerpiece of the human race and the Leader of the column of progress.
>
> I am far within the mark when I say that all the armies that ever marched, and all the navies that ever were built, and all the parliaments that ever sat, and all the kings that ever reigned, put together have not affected the life of man upon this earth as powerfully as has that one solitary Life.

The young man, obviously impressed, said quietly, "That's it—that's the missing piece in the puzzle."

D. *In Touch with God*

At this point his spiritual guide remarked that the business of surrendering to this Christ meant such simple but exacting things as: (1) the confessed willingness to be done with sin in every known form; (2) the purpose to pray and to keep in touch with God continuously; (3) openness to God's will in the investment of one's life, particularly as regards vocation, marriage, and other important concerns; and (4) the commitment to win others to Christ and to the Christian life.

What followed belongs to the true "confessional" of the Gospel. He really wanted Christ now, was ruthlessly honest with himself and with God concerning his sins; and, though he had never prayed aloud with anyone before, he got on his knees and poured out his soul in a quiet torrent of confession, including one particularly evil thing that had occurred during the war and had left its hideous scar upon his conscience.

When he got to his feet, his eyes were shining!

Almost immediately he told his fiancée about his new faith and experience. The wedding that followed was permeated with the spirit of Christ. This was followed by his announcement that he was even willing to give serious consideration to going into full-time Christian service if that should be God's will.

What a swift journey he had taken into the land of spiritual discovery! And what a land it is! It is costly to enter, but it is worth it!

And now one thing follows.

III. Two QUESTS—AND EACH OF THEM, ENDING IN A COSTLY SURRENDER, PRODUCES AN EXTRAORDINARY SATISFACTION

Take it first in God's case. I hope you are not finicky about it, thinking that perhaps it is out of place to speak of God as One who derives satisfaction from the results of His search for man. The prophet had said, concerning the Suffering Servant—Jesus—that He should "see of the travail of his soul, and shall be satisfied" (Isa. 53:11).

A. *One Missing*

Surely none of us can forget the picture of the Shepherd that Jesus drew for us. Ninety-nine sheep in the fold and one missing! What then? "There's just one thing for it," says Jesus. He turns His back on the ninety and nine to "go after that which is lost, until he find it. And when he hath found it, he layeth it on his shoulders, rejoicing" (Luke 15:4, 5). So great is His satisfaction that, according to Jesus, "when he cometh home, he calleth together his friends and neighbors, saying unto them, Rejoice with me; for I have found my sheep which was lost" (v. 6).

God revels in that kind of satisfaction.

And what of those who find Him in Christ? They too experience a satisfaction that is deep and elemental and, in the fullest sense, indescribable. For satisfaction, mind you, is a far deeper thing than *pleasure,* or *relief,* or *escape,* or *stimulation.* You can get these from money, or art, or fame, or human love.

But satisfaction comes from knowing, here and now, that you are harmonized with God, that you are at home in His universe, that what you have in Christ has eternal meaning and value. Money may vanish, art may fade, friends may fail, health may pale, death may reach relentlessly for the valves of the heart. No matter! You are Christ's and Christ is yours— forever!

B. *Sufficient for Life and Death*

Dr. James Stalker told of a gifted young Scot who graduated with honors from a Scottish university and went out to Australia to teach mathematics. But he hadn't been there long when his health failed. It was clear that he wouldn't live. So he returned to die among his native Scottish hills. One lovely September afternoon, shortly before the end, he was driven out on the moors for "just another look at the heather." As they started, he pointed to two of his acquaint-

A vast amount of material relative to the death of our Lord is available for the Palm Sunday and Good Friday season: the inexhaustible passion narratives of the four Gospels (one-third of the entire Gospel of John is devoted to a record of the last eight days of Christ's life on earth, from Palm Sunday to Easter Sunday) ; the great types and prophecies relating to the death of Christ in the Old Testament; Christ's own predictions about His death; the extended passages in the epistles of the New Testament which interpret the atoning and reconciling work of the Son of God; and the innumerable passages in the Book of Revelation which speak of the eternal consequences of His holy death.

Choosing to give a series of expository sermons on any one book of the Bible will relieve the minister, for a time, of the necessity of selecting a text from which to preach week by week. For two years Dr. Martyn Lloyd-Jones held his large Sunday morning congregations at Westminster Chapel, London, with sixty successive messages from the first two chapters of the Epistle to the Ephesians, and he is now covering the next two chapters with equal thoroughness. Relief from concern over a text from which to preach is also experienced when we choose to bring a series on some general theme in the Word of God—the parables, prominent characters of divine revelation, the questions asked of Jesus, the prayers of the Bible, etc. Then, there is that blessed experience, which should be ours frequently, of earnestly pleading with God to direct us to the text on which we should preach. All truly sincere ministers will testify to the fact that sometimes it is necessary to spend more time before the Lord seeking guidance in a subject to preach on than is later required in preparing that sermon, once we have been divinely led to a specific text.

In regard to the choice of texts, I should like to make three suggestions. First of all, we should not, because of laziness or some other excuse, avoid the profound passages

ances a few paces away, and said to his companion, "What do you think they have been talking about all morning? Sartor Resartus!" (It is anything but a cheap and evil book.) Still, with strange wistfulness and that kind of seriousness that comes from peering into eternity, he went on: "That is not what a dying man wants. 'This is a faithful saying, and worthy of all acceptation, that Christ Jesus came into the world to save sinners.' That is what a dying man wants!"

Yes, that *is* what a dying man wants! Or any man!

> In life, in death, in sorrow and in sinning,
>   Christ will suffice me, for He hath sufficed;
> Christ is the end, for Christ is the beginning,
>   Christ is the beginning, for the end is Christ.

WILBUR MOOREHEAD SMITH

Born in Chicago, Illinois, in 1894.

Moody Bible Institute, 1913-14; College of Wooster, Ohio, 1914-17; D.D., Evangelical Theological College, Dallas, Texas.

Ordained Presbyterian ministry, 1922; pastor, Lafayette Square Presbyterian Church, Baltimore, 1922-27; First Presbyterian Church, Covington, Virginia, 1927-30; Presbyterian Church of Coatesville, Pennsylvania, 1930-37; member faculty of Moody Bible Institute, Chicago, Illinois, 1938-47.

Professor, English Bible, Fuller Theological Seminary, Pasadena, California, 1947—; editor, *Peloubet's Select Notes* on the International Sunday School Lessons since 1933; member, American Society of Church History, Society of Biblical Literature and Exegesis, Victoria Institute, London, England. Conference speaker.

Author: *The Supernaturalness of Christ; Therefore Stand; This Atomic Age and the Word of God; The Approaching World Crisis; The Word of God and The Life of Holiness; Profitable Bible Study; Egypt in Biblical Prophecy;* and others.

No Set Rules

IT IS INEVITABLE that men of differing temperaments and habits and varying educational backgrounds will have different methods of preparing sermons, and the methods used by one able preacher may cramp the style of another man equally able. There is no set of rules which every minister must follow. What I am about to say (and this is the first time in my life I have ever attempted to write on this subject) is not a collection of theories, but a simple state-

ment of the method I have pursued through the ye may be that I should have chosen some more effective od, but it is too late now to change.

THE CHOICE OF SUBJECTS AND TEXTS

The method used in preparing a sermon will often de upon how we have been led to choose some particular Occasionally in the reading of a chapter in a book divo from sermon preparation, a text will stand out and so g us that we are compelled to preach on it the following S day. I remember as a young minister reading Dr. G. Cam bell Morgan's volume on Hosea, *The Heart and Holiness God,* and being overwhelmed by his masterly interpretatio of the phrase: "I will give the valley of Achor for a door o hope" (2:15). Again—and this should not be too often—on feels compelled to find textual materials for preaching on a subject that is occupying the thoughts of men across the nation, or perhaps around the world, some national disaster or outstanding scientific discovery or achievement. Any minister who has an acquaintance with the prophetic writings of the Word of God would certainly recognize these last few months as an opportune time for speaking to his people of the significance of celestial phenomena in Biblical prophecy (which, let me hasten to add, I am sure has no reference to Sputnik or the Explorer). When some crushing sorrow has come to a family or group of people in the church which may raise questions and doubts in the minds of fellow believers, the minister must find help for them in the Word of God.

The church calendar will frequently lead the faithful pastor to preach on some aspect of the season being celebrated. It would not be out of order to devote two or three Sunday mornings and evenings before Christmas to some of the glorious themes of the nativity narratives. The Sunday preceding New Year's Day is an opportune time to speak from some text in which the words *new, renew,* or *regeneration* occur.

of the Word of God, the theological passages: in other words, we must never devote that sacred hour in the pulpit to some superficial sermonette on a line from the Scriptures which in itself cannot possibly have any real spiritual significance. I recall returning from a vacation, while pastor of a church in the East, and learning that the visiting minister, a relative of one of the members, had dared to preach on the phrase "a basket of summer fruit" (Amos 1) in his one sermon of the entire week. He did little more than describe summer fruits, oranges, lemons, bananas, etc. How tragic!

Second (and here I personally have been at fault), in the light of Paul's exhortation to rightly divide the Word of truth, we should endeavor, in a ministry covering a considerable length of time in one church, to preach from every major portion of the Word of God, or at least from every book in the Bible. My faithful pastor in Chicago, the late Dr. Henry Hepburn, kept a card index of the texts of his sermons, and when he found that he was preaching too often from one or two books, to the exclusion of others, he would abandon that section for a time and set himself the task of preparing a sermon or two from some books which he had been neglecting.

Finally, a minister should keep a list of sermon subjects on which some day he will want to preach; if possible, texts should be attached to these subjects. When leaving the pastorate to become a teacher, I had at least 140 subjects listed in a notebook on which I wanted to preach. Occasionally I look at this list and realize that in subsequent years I have spoken on some of these topics, but not because they were there. It is well to keep mulling over certain profound passages in the Word of God, for the day will come when suddenly the passage will burst forth in full flowering, and then one has a sermon—the result of years of meditation. As an illustration, I have been looking at Daniel 2 for many years. Every time I teach the Book of Daniel, I am again drawn to the text—one of the greatest prayers in all the Bible. But as yet I have not felt equipped to preach on it.

THE STUDY OF A CHOSEN TEXT

We shall confine ourselves to texts from the New Testament, for generally the principles apply also to Old Testament texts. I think I will not be misunderstood in saying that there are some texts in the New Testament which really do not need careful investigation in the original Greek, e.g., the words of our Lord to Matthew: "And as Jesus passed forth from thence, he saw a man, named Matthew, sitting at the receipt of custom: and he saith unto him, Follow me. And he arose, and followed him" (9:9). Generally speaking, however, one should first carefully examine the words of the Greek text, particularly of the New Testament Epistles. Magnificent material is available for this today. The great theological Lexicon by Cremer is still of value, as is the later, and for many years indispensable, work by Thayer, but now we also have the finest single-volume lexicon that has appeared in the English language, Bauer's *Greek-English Lexicon of the New Testament,* revised by Arndt and Gingrich. This throws light upon the vocabulary of the Greek Testament from the papyri and the later discoveries in early Christian literature, and contains excellent bibliographies. In addition, one will find help in Baxter's *Englishman's Concordance to the Greek New Testament,* the virtues of which need not be set forth here. New Testament words in the Septuagint comprise a rich source of material; for this see the Redpath and Hatch *Concordance to the Greek Old Testament.* For such word study, there is still the precious volume by Archbishop Trench, *New Testament Synonyms.*

To illustrate this particular type of study, let us take the Greek word *koomos,* translated "rioting" or "reveling" (Rom. 13:13; Gal. 5:21; I Peter 4:3). What could be more illuminating than the following definition and interpretation in Thayer: "A revel, carousel; in Greek writers, a nocturnal and riotous procession of half-drunken and frolicsome fellows who after supper parade through the streets with torches and music in honor of Bacchus or some other deity, and sing and play before their male and female friends; hence, generally of feasts and drinking parties that are protracted until late at night and indulge in revelry." In his *Synonyms,* Trench has this interesting comment, "The shame involved in what this word stood for in Paul's day is universally prevalent in this twentieth century." Don't forget that Alexander Maclaren, G. Campbell Morgan, and many other outstanding preachers of the last quarter-century were constant students of the Greek New Testament, and even of Greek grammar.

Having grasped the meaning of the words contained in the text, I try to put myself into the mood of the one from whom these words proceeded, and the occasion which prompted them. I read the best commentaries, confining this, for the most part, to commentaries on the Greek text— and I must not yield to the temptation to mention some of them here. May I urge young ministers, with all fervor, to shun these so-called homiletical helps; they are only crutches. One can become so dependent upon them that he loses his ability to approach a text independently, and becomes simply the mouthpiece for other men's thoughts, not allowing God to speak through him some particular message for that hour. When students come to me to ask if they should purchase some set of thirty volumes of homiletical helps, I immediately reply in the negative. It is a waste of time to read this literature, and it paralyzes one's divinely bestowed gift for interpreting the Word of God.

When all the material available on a text had been gathered, and I had given it all the additional thought of which I was capable, I would arrange my notes in outline form. Without an outline, no sermon is worth preaching. Observe the method of outlining used by Dr. G. Campbell Morgan in his books, *The Crises of the Christ* and *The Teaching of Christ*. After one has drawn up an outline and knows the way he is moving, he can afford to read three or four great sermons on the text, but, I repeat, this should not be done until *after* an original outline has been completed. As Sir William Robertson Nicoll once said of the sermons of Alexander Maclaren: "If we were reading a sermon of Maclaren on a text we were about to preach from, so perfect would we find Maclaren's outline, we would either have to accept his outline or get another text."

Perhaps a word should be said here about personal contribution to the development of a sermon. The more richly we live, the more valuable our sermons should be. This enrichment of life can be enhanced by wide reading, reading day and night, every spare moment—and some moments we cannot spare—by our continual contacts with others, our pastoral visits, experiences with other Christian leaders, and personal spiritual experiences, though we must not be autobiographical in the pulpit too frequently. I would be almost tempted to say that we might draw upon our travels for sermonic illustrations, but that kind of travel would have to be across the water, not here. One shudders when he hears, as I did recently, of a minister returning from vacation and preaching a series of sermons on some road signs he had seen, one of which was, "The pause that refreshes." I am not so sure that an audience will be in a mood for something from the Word of God when their minds are on Coca-Cola.

Illustrations, if good, can be one of the most valuable parts of a sermon. A master in the use of illustration was Dr. Harry Ironside. I can still remember some that I heard from him thirty years ago. Dr. Jowett had people reading for him in different parts of the world, and his illustrations were superb. On the other hand, Dr. G. Campbell Morgan used very few illustrations: it was solid meat from the first sentence to the last, but he held audiences spellbound. May I caution young men to be wary of accumulating books of illustrations and then, when preaching on humility, for example, search these pages for an account of some act of humility, coming away with a story of some obscure character in the days of the Puritans which will mean nothing to the modern congregation. The more illustrations we can glean from our own reading and intercourse with others, the fresher our sermons will be. Normally an illustration taken from a book of illustrations leaves a taste of staleness, and many times such illustrations are trivial.

WORKING WITH PENCIL AND PEN

May I refer here to a very practical aspect of sermon preparation, what might be called hack work. I must work with pen or pencil. My thoughts are expressed through these instruments of recording. When beginning work on a sermon, I reach first for a pad of paper, 8½" x 11", and fill the page or pages with notes from my reading and thought on the text. This completed, I take another sheet and outline the text, inserting my materials under these divisions. When I have thus gathered and classified everything, the sermon is outlined on 4" x 6" white cards. Any sentences to be quoted are written out in full, with the references, and verses of Scripture to be used in illuminating the chosen text. Personally, I am not skilled in speaking extemporaneously from a text: I must think it through and know which way I am moving. Introductions and conclusions to messages must sometimes wait for final decision, and this decision may not come until frighteningly late. There are all kinds of introductions and conclusions, and I must not dwell on that now, but there must be some way of bringing the message forcefully to a close.

Finally, there is the minister's Saturday night. I would let nothing interfere with my being in the study from seven to ten o'clock Saturday night, without interruption. A minister could well doom himself to failure in the pulpit by allowing Saturday evenings to be spent in social intercourse with the members of his church, or even in pastoral visitation, unless it is an emergency. It may seem strange to some, but at ten o'clock on Saturday night, I have not hesitated to go to the home where my wife has been visiting—so that she could leave me in the house alone—and to have a half hour of quiet social fellowship, to relieve the strain of long preparation. Of course, one will want to return to the sermon Sunday morning, in whatever time he might have. Thousands of ministers across the country will know what I mean when I say that over and over again, after my sermon has been finished, I have not been satisfied as to how to apply it to the hearts of my people the next day, or even how to conclude it. At the last moment God has given me some truth relative to the text—more pertinent than anything resulting from a week of labor on the subject.

I know of no quick road to worth-while preaching. It is hard work, but wonderfully rewarding. We are living in a day of superficial, inconsequential, unmoving preaching. I trust that anyone who reads these pages will ask God to deliver him from the temptation to live in this type of homiletical poverty and dullness. Unless our souls are painfully exercised and we know what it is to wrestle with God and to contend with principalities and powers, we will never be able to move the souls of others.

Life—Through Jesus Christ

Wilbur Moorehead Smith

IN THE FOURTH GOSPEL, we have one of the few occasions recorded in the Word of God where the author of a book tells why he wrote it. John said: "These are written that ye may believe that Jesus is the Christ the Son of God, and that believing ye may have life through his name." Whatever this verse may mean—and we shall look at it in a moment—I would assume that John was successful in what he undertook. Many authors are not; that is, a man starts out to write a book, and the work falls flat: he either does not accomplish his purpose, or he is not able to write in a style that holds the attention of the reader, or the book is full of errors and faults, or he himself is ignorant and had no business writing on the subject—and there is more than one case like that. Indeed, I suppose that anyone who does any writing feels that he never reaches the power and clarity that he wishes he could command.

First of all the apostle John was under the inspiration of the Holy Spirit and divinely guided in what he was doing. And the book itself, with its marvelous depths, its beauty of expression, and the unforgettable pages that have come down through the ages, bears testimony that John did succeed in his purpose. Oh, how many, because of this book, *have* believed that Jesus is the Christ the Son of God! The famous historian Schaff says that the Gospel of John is the most influential book that has ever come from the pen of any man, and I would not be a bit surprised if in Heaven there will be great multitudes of people who have been saved through some verse from John's Gospel, the result of his writing that men might believe.

Now, as we look at this text, I would like to take one phrase from the middle that has nothing religious in it at all—nothing about the Lord, nothing about God—and begin with that—"that . . . ye may have life." Everyone on this earth has life, some kind of life. In this country we have *abundant* life. Think of the vigor and the strength that most Americans are able to display. People coming over here from England are astonished at the hurry, the rush, the energy, and the fervor of men at work. We have life: we have intellectual life; we have physical life. But John cannot be writing about that kind of life. There is nothing in John's Gospel that will give that kind of life if we do not have it. Everyone living on this earth has biological life. When John says: "These things have I written that ye may have *life*," he is referring to something different from the mere life that is in our veins, in the blood of our bodies, the life that throbs in these mental processes, and the emotional life of our hearts. We must look through the Gospel to find what John really meant by this word *life*.

Let's take the most famous of all statements referring to life: "God so loved the world, that he gave his only begotten Son, that whosoever believeth in him should not perish, but have everlasting [eternal] life." That kind of life no man has in the blood of his veins: he does not get that from his father and mother. *Eternal life,* that is, life that goes on forever and ever, in all of its glory and wonder, is something in which I would say the larger number of people on earth do not even believe. Most scientists believe, I am sorry to say, that when the body dies, and goes back into dust, nothing will ever remain of anything that lived in that body, neither soul nor anything else. With the exception of those in the church, millions in Soviet Russia believe that there is no life yet to come, there is no God, there is no Heaven, there is no future. The great mass of people—as you and I ought to be aware of and seldom are—do not even believe that there is such a life.

The Gospel continually points to and promises this higher, divinely bestowed life. The Lord Jesus affirmed, "I am the resurrection and the life." This is the kind of life that our mother and father could never give us. I am grateful that my father passed on to me a strong body, and a passion for work. Some parents have passed on to some of you artistic abilities, a handsome countenance, or a beautiful face. But no father and no mother can ever pass on to a child the life that is in God, this life that is in the Lord Jesus, this life that emancipates from sin, this life that satisfies, that bestows the peace of God that passeth all understanding, life that brings us to the throne of grace, the life that ultimately will take us into the presence of the Lord Jesus. "In my Father's house are many mansions. I go to prepare a place for you, and if I go and prepare a place for you, I will come again and receive you unto myself, that where I am there ye may be also." This is the life that the apostle John is talking about. "These things are written that ye may have *life*"—divine life, the life that is in Christ.

We must now examine the context of this promise of eternal life. "Many other signs truly did Jesus in the presence of his disciples which are not written in this book, but these are written that ye might believe that Jesus is"—I want to stop right there—"that ye might believe that Jesus is . . ." We must start with this. The way for you and me, and any man or woman on this earth, to obtain and appropriate this life that is in God, this eternal, abundant, satisfying life, is not by becoming proficient in languages, by being literate, by developing artistic skills, by getting into some social register, or *Who's Who*, by joining some political party, by hard work, by some philosophic system, by following some lofty ideal, by getting a college degree, by doing good—none of that is here, valuable as these things are in themselves. When John says "that we may have life," he is pointing to a Person; this life is in Him, and can be received only from Him. Let us return to the full verse: "These things are written that ye might believe that Jesus is the Christ the Son of God." I don't see how any man, honestly, in his right mind can deny that there was a Jesus on this earth. When I made a poll last year among scientists on the belief in the resurrection, I admit I had three or four letters from well-known men with scientific degrees, who expressed their doubt that Jesus ever lived. Also I know that the Russian *Soviet Encyclopedia* declares that this man Jesus never lived. But, we all know that this is A.D. 1958, which is *anno Domini, the year of our Lord,* and that we cannot date Caesar's invasion of Britain, or Gaul, without placing after those figures the letters B.C., *before Christ.* Someone came into history so powerful, so convulsive in what He did and said, that He cut history right in two: every event occurring before the advent of Jesus is designated B.C., and everything since the coming of the Lord Jesus is dated A.D. Every cross you see on every steeple, every institution truly called a church, every communion table you ever behold, every sacramental feast in which we ever participate, any preaching of the Gospel, any opening of the New Testament, any identification of a person by the word *Christian*—all point to one fact, that in Galilee, in the first century, born of Mary in Bethlehem, living in Nazareth, dying in Jerusalem, there was a Man on this earth called Jesus who went about doing good, who spake as no other man spake.

John is not writing to prove that Jesus lived, but rather is writing to prove something about this man Jesus. Notice what he says: "But these are written that ye might believe that Jesus is"—now something follows that has been true of no one else living in these six thousand years of human history, and will not be true of anyone else if history should last sixty thousand more years—and the way it looks now, it could end in sixty thousand more hours! "These are written that ye might believe that Jesus is . . ." May I interrupt? The other day I acquired the large *Jewish Encyclopedia* in twelve volumes, published about forty years ago. You will find here the name *Jesus* on every third or fourth page, and even a long article on Jesus. You will come upon some statements about our Lord in the article on the Pharisees, and on the Sadducees, in the section on Jerusalem, and in the sketch of John the Baptist. Jesus interpenetrates the whole encyclopedia. I suppose there is not a reasonable Jew on earth who doesn't believe there was a Jesus. John is not writing to prove that fact to the Jews. "These are written that ye may believe that Jesus is the Christ the Son of God."

In this word *Christ* we have the Hebrew word *Messiah,* meaning "the sent one of God, the anointed one of God." What was it that Nathanael said, and Philip? "We have found the Messiah of whom Moses and the prophets did speak." This is the Seed of the woman prophesied in Genesis. This is the One who will rule the nations, as Jacob said on his deathbed in Genesis 49. This is that great Teacher like unto Moses whom God was to send, declared to and by Moses. This is the One, the Lamb led to the slaughter, who would carry our sins and lay down His life for us, as foretold by Isaiah. This is the virgin-born One! This is the King promised to David, the High Priest like unto Melchizedek, spoken of in the Psalms. This is He of whom Moses and the prophets did speak, says John. Then, he adds, this One is also the Son of God—*the* Son of God. Beloved, we are so accustomed to this phrase that it hardly rings a bell with us. But imagine opening a paper tomorrow morning and seeing on the front page the statement that the British parliament had passed a resolution that the greatest man in Britain today, and the greatest man Britain has known since the days of Gladstone, Winston Churchill, is now declared to be the Son of God.

What a shudder would go across the whole Western world, in response to such blasphemy! I remember during World War II when the Japanese emperor announced that he was not divine—and *that* we could all believe. But for any mere man to say that he is *the Son of God*—you and I just wouldn't believe it, because we would know it was not true. Every man on this earth has had a father and mother, was born at a certain time, did not have any existence at all a year before birth, and is doomed to die, and rest in a grave. Jesus said, "I came down from my Father." Let any man say that to you tomorrow, and you would begin to doubt his sanity. The Lord said, "Before Abraham was, I am." These are astonishing assertions. Then He said, "The Father and I are one." And the Jews took up stones to kill Him.

Now I want to go back to this text: "These are written that ye may believe that Jesus [the historic Jesus] is the Messiah, the Son of God." Do you believe that? Over and over again I read that men are saying, "I love the teachings of Jesus"; "I think He has given us a good ethic"; "He set us a wonderful example"; "I just want more of the spirit of Jesus"; and then, in the next breath, they insist that He is not divine, and that He lives in His spirit, but is dead in His body! That is not the way the New Testament reads. There is no divine life, God's life, eternal life, abundant life, apart from this cardinal truth that Jesus is the Christ, the Son of God. This is borne in upon me more and more as I get older, and it is a terrible thing, and a glorious thing. The destiny of every man who ever hears the Gospel is determined by what he thinks about Jesus Christ. I repeat—the destiny of every man who hears the Gospel is determined by what he thinks of Jesus Christ.

Our text says: "Many other signs truly did Jesus in the presence of his disciples, which are not written in this book." In his Gospel, John gives the events of not more than thirty days in Christ's public ministry, which covered something over twelve hundred days, and some of these chapters, for example chapter 11, are wholly taken up with one single miracle, out of the hundreds that our Lord performed; so that John can say: "Many *other* signs truly did Jesus in the presence of his disciples, which are not written in this book, but these are written that ye may believe." What were the signs—a word for miracles—in John's Gospel which are written that we might believe? There are seven of them. I'm going to name them, and not expound them. In the second chapter, the turning of water into wine; in the fourth chapter, the healing of the nobleman's son; in the fifth chapter, the healing of the impotent man who was paralyzed; in the sixth chapter, the first section, the feeding of the five thousand, and the second section, the walking of Jesus on the water; in the ninth chapter, the healing of the man born blind; and finally, in the eleventh chapter, the raising of Lazarus. Surely we are living in a wonderful age, nineteen hundred years after Jesus died, and we have a marvelous mastery of many phenomena that were not even discussed in the days of our Lord.

But where on this earth today is the man who with a word —using no chemical liquid or similar substance—can change large earthen jars of water into good wine? Where is the man who can take a person who has been paralyzed for forty years and with one word cause that man to take up his bed and walk? Where is the scientist today who can take a handful of little fishes and a few small loaves, and continue breaking them until he feeds five thousand people? Where is the man who can go to a tomb where a body has begun to disintegrate, and call that one by name and bring him out whole?

Nineteen hundred and fifty years have gone by since Jesus of Nazareth walked the streets of Jerusalem and the highways of Galilee. These things He did are still miracles. It would have been altogether different had He stood in a chariot, ordinarily drawn by slaves or horses, and said, "Take that beast out of those shafts, I'll get down from Nazareth to

Jerusalem in a way that you don't understand." You would say, "Well, that was wonderful then, but Henry Ford can do it now." But Jesus didn't do that. Our Lord did not sit out under the Syrian stars one night with the disciples and, asking if they would like to hear a debate in the Roman Forum, turn some knob on an instrument and bring in the debate by radio. You would say, "That's all right, but we know how to do that now too."

As we continue looking at these miracles, what do we discover? That Jesus had mastery over nature, that He had mastery over disease, that He has absolute mastery over death, and that He has complete mastery of what we call matter (so that He can break up a little item and multiply it sufficiently to meet the dietary needs of five thousand people). He has mastery over nature, over matter, over disease, and over death—no one else has ever walked this earth with such mastery and power.

But there is something else here. All these things were for what purpose?—for good. I was reading the life of J. D. Jones, of Bournemouth, one of England's outstanding preachers, recently deceased. In this volume is a quotation from a letter of Jones, who was world-famous, regarding a colleague of his in Divinity at Cambridge who went off to a small church and stayed there for thirty-five years, never widely known, just going on doing his work. Jones wrote, "That man [and he called him by name] Clayton had the greatest virtue given to men—he was good!" He said, "His goodness at Cambridge cleansed all of our lives, and the very remembrance of my friend Clayton has a beneficent effect upon my soul even today; he was good." Our Lord had power, and He was divine, but supremely, He went about doing good! And everywhere He went, He labored for the needs of men and women, loving others and forgetting self. "These things are written that ye may believe that Jesus is the Christ the Son of God." I would like to ask you, Do you believe that?

You recall John the Baptist, greatest prophet of that century certainly, the first after four hundred years, who lived that separated, Spirit-filled life out there in the wilderness, until the whole city of Jerusalem came out to hear him speak. "There cometh one after me," he said, "whose shoe latchet I am not worthy to unloose." "I saw," he declared later, "the Spirit descending as a dove upon him, and I heard a voice from heaven saying, This is my beloved Son in whom I am well pleased." That was his verdict. And what is the testimony of John the apostle, next to Paul, the most profound thinker in theology of the first century? Listen to John's opening words: "In the beginning was the Word, and the Word was with God, and the Word was God. . . . All things were made by him and without him was not anything made that was made. . . . And the Word became flesh and dwelt among us, and we beheld his glory, the glory as of the only begotten of the Father, full of grace and truth." Nathanael said: "Thou art the Christ, the Son of the living God." The Samaritans, hated by the Jews, looking on this Jewish Jesus, Son of David, said: "Now we believe that this is indeed the Christ, the Saviour of the world." Skeptical Thomas could look at the Lord and cry out, "My Lord and my God." And God Himself spoke from Heaven three times: "This is my beloved Son, hear ye him."

"He that believeth on the Son hath life, and he that believeth not the Son of God shall not see life." "I am the resurrection and the life. . . . Believest thou this?" "God so loved the world" (that's wonderful) "that he gave his only begotten Son" (and that's also wonderful) "that whosoever believeth in him" (that's open enough and wide enough) "shall not perish" (that's a terrible word—and we quote this verse so glibly) "but have *everlasting* life." My dear people, if there was ever a time since you and I were born that no man has known what the next day would bring forth, this is the time. We can be sure of nothing, nothing, except what

we have in Christ. "For neither life nor death, nor principalities, nor powers, nor things present nor things to come
shall ever separate us from the love of God which is in Christ
Jesus our Lord." In closing, I want to ask a simple question,
Do you believe that Jesus is the Christ the Son of God? In
believing, you have life, everlasting life, in His name.

J. R. W. STOTT

Born in London, 1921.

Educated Rugby School, Trinity College, Cambridge (Modern and Medieval Languages Tripos Part I—French 1st class, German 2nd class; Theological Tripos Part I, 1st class; senior scholar 1944); Ridley Hall, Cambridge.

Ordained as curate to All Souls Langham Place with St. Peter's Vere Street in 1945, and was appointed Rector in 1950. Student and Conference speaker of International reputation.

Author: *Men with a Message,* the Bishop of London's Lent Book for 1954, an examination of the distinctive themes of the New Testament authors.

Stewards of God

M Y FIRST AND DEEPEST CONVICTION about preaching is that a minister is never more than the steward of goods entrusted to him and the herald of news which he has been commanded to proclaim. Therefore he is never the originator of new ideas, but only the dispenser of old. His task is simply to explain, to interpret, and to apply God's revealed and written Word. This brings me to the first stage of which I am conscious in preparing a sermon: choosing the subject.

CHOOSING THE SUBJECT

Granted that my textbook is the Bible, a lifetime is not long enough to explore and describe all its territory. How then shall I decide each Sunday which particular text from

179

the Book to expound? In some ways this is my biggest head-
ache, not from lack of material but from the very abundance
of it. My plan (by no means always realized in practice, I
am afraid) is to begin on Monday afternoon to make next
Sunday's selection. It is then a great help to meditate on
the theme during the week. I try therefore to keep Monday
afternoons free. I retire to a quiet room in the house and
seek in prayer to discover God's will for the subject of next
Sunday's sermons. I find I am often guided by three considerations.

Personal. The lessons which God has been teaching me in
my own Christian life form the most natural subject for
transmission to others. Of course sometimes one is called
to preach objectively on themes of which one has no personal
experience. One may preach on suffering, for instance, before one has suffered, and one is obliged to preach on death
before one has died! But it is easier and often safer to lead
the congregation along paths which one is treading. It is
essential to write down at once any particularly luminous
thoughts which the Holy Spirit puts into my mind. I forget
them if I do not record them at once. My own daily times
of Bible reading morning and evening are always the most
fruitful from this point of view. I keep two loose-leaf note-
books, one textual in Biblical order (Genesis to Revelation)
and the other topical (indexed under headings), in which
I record what I learn. Sometimes it is only a verse and a
thought, and sometimes the analysis of a long chapter or the
development of a whole theme. Each of these entries is the
seed from which a sermon may later sprout.

Congregational. The second source of ideas for sermon
subjects is the need of the congregation which I serve. Talks
with church members on their spiritual problems, in visit or
interview, continually reveal that they are confused about
some doctrine or negligent of some Christian practice. Apart
from such immediate needs I try to keep a watchful eye on

what is preached throughout the year, in order to ensure that each year some Biblical instruction is given on all the major aspects of Christian belief and behavior. Otherwise I find that some of the more difficult subjects tend to be omitted! Two or three times a year I plan courses of sermons, and this arrangement greatly facilitates earlier and more thorough preparation.

National. Other sermon subjects are suggested to me by what is going on in the life of the nation. My fellow countrymen may be celebrating some religious season (Christmas, Easter, Whitsun, etc.) or some historical anniversary. The newspapers may be featuring some disaster or tragedy which invites a frank and courageous sermon on divine providence and human suffering. Or there may at the time be public discussion of moral issues like Sunday observance, vice, gambling, and the racial question. Alternatively, the Christian press may be concentrating on some particular question like Biblical authority or interchurch relations on which the congregation would value guidance. I find my shallow thinking being continually challenged. Am I to shirk these problems or grapple with them? Is the Church to be out of touch with life, or can the Word of God be related to the happenings of the day?

STUDYING THE TEXT

When the subject is chosen, it is not usually difficult to be led to the appropriate scriptural passage. Indeed, often the one suggests the other. To me every sermon should be expository, whether the text is a few words, a verse, a paragraph, a chapter or even a book. Christian people find it a help not only to share the microscopic study of an isolated sentence, but to be introduced to some of the grand themes of God's Word and to grasp the message of whole books. Whatever text is selected, the careful study of it is the second stage of my sermon preparation. I begin by reading it, rereading it,

and reading it again. I look at the original text and wrestle
with it until it yields its meaning. I read it in various translations and paraphrases. I meditate on it prayerfully and seek
to discover its implications and applications. Meanwhile, I
am writing down (in unself-conscious confusion) all the
thoughts which come into my mind. When, after perhaps a
considerable time, I feel I have sucked the text dry, I turn to
the commentaries and note down any further ideas they
may give me. As I go on, some kind of order begins to emerge
from the chaos of material before me. God seems to lay
upon me some principal aim and object in the sermon, to
which other ideas must become subordinate. The subject
appears to divide itself into distinct sections or aspects, and
a framework is built. I normally look for suitable headings
for each point, preferably between two and four, but I am
no great lover of alliteration unless it is both natural and
helpful. Once the main purpose and the general framework
of the sermon have been settled, the third stage begins.

Shaping the Material

Apart from the headings, the sermon is still a mass of clay
waiting to be shaped. In the process much waste will have to
be discarded. I confess I do not find it easy to be as ruthless
as I should be in rejecting material which is not strictly relevant to the sermon's theme. But this must be done. All the
time I am thinking to myself: "God has given me a subject
and a congregation; how can I communicate *it* to *them?*"
Some of the people may be ignorant, prejudiced, sleepy, or
deceived. How can the truth be conveyed to them so that
they grasp it, apply it, remember it, and go out to live by it?
Now comes the fascination of bridge-building, of conveying
the traffic of truth safely across from my mind (where God
has temporarily parked it) into their minds (its destination)?
I know no way but by painstaking labor. By preliminary
study I have come to understand the passage. But now I must

patiently and prayerfully search for ways and means to express it with limpid clarity and pungent forcefulness—now with a memorable epigram, now with an illuminating illustration, now with a touch of humor, now with a series of short, sharp sentences, driving in a point like hammer blows on a nail, now with a vivid metaphor which fires the imagination.

I am a great believer in the need to extend our preparation to the very words we use. To be sure, the Holy Spirit can give us words in the pulpit, and if we have a script, we shall be free to depart from it, but He can give us words in our study too. It is so easy to become slipshod in preparation and rationalize our laziness by pious talk about the Holy Spirit! We believe the Holy Spirit took great trouble in the selection of His words in Scripture. We must do the same. Words matter. A striking combination of words can pierce the armor of a closed mind, when flabby platitudes cannot. To spend time on the choice of words helps to enrich our vocabulary, forces us to think and express ourselves clearly, and delivers a settled congregation from the boredom which our monotonous clichés often inspire.

Having sought to shape the body of the sermon, I finish with the head and tail. The introduction must arrest the attention of the people, and at the same time introduce the subject in such a way that they want to listen carefully to the rest. The conclusion must be as down to earth as most tails are! The time for explanation and interpretation is over; the time for application has come. Personally I find this difficult, but I know its importance. It is possible for a congregation to fathom the meaning of a sermon and never feel its impact. They can go home untouched, unwounded, and uncomforted. Somehow the sermon must penetrate their hearts and move their sluggish wills. Somehow the listeners, varied as their needs are, must go away resolved to translate what they have heard into immediate and practical action.

Writing the Sermon

I now have before me a bundle of papers illegible enough to intimidate even him who is expert in the deciphering of ancient scripts! There are inkings in and crossings out, lines and circles and arrows of every shape and size. A fair copy seems to be indicated. I still believe that the ideal method is to write or type the sermon in full, and then make notes for use in the pulpit. I did this myself when I began. I wish I still did. But the exigencies of time have led me to a compromise. I make a very full summary, which I also take into the pulpit. It is so full that it includes whole sentences more or less verbatim, but by the use of abbreviations it can be compressed into cards measuring 5″ x 3″. I underline main headings and paragraph beginnings, so that I do not get lost. I find that by preparing a very carefully chiseled rough draft, writing its summary on a card, and then looking it through on my knees before preaching it, the sermon is so fixed in my memory that I can preach it freely without either reading it off the back of my mind or being tied to my script.

The cards are punched with two holes so that I can put them into a loose-leaf book for pulpit use. I then file them in a steel cabinet of drawers, under either Scripture references or topical subjects. I write on both sides of these cards, except for the first card of each sermon on the back of which I write the place at which it has been preached and the date. Illustrations, and quotations from books read, I put on the same cards. These can then easily be slipped into my loose-leaf book with any sermon for which I need them.

The Exaltation of Jesus

J. R. W. STOTT

Wherefore also God highly exalted him, and gave unto him the name which is above every name; that in the name of Jesus every knee should bow . . . in heaven and . . . on earth and . . . under the earth, and that every tongue should confess that Jesus Christ is Lord, to the glory of God the Father (Phil. 2:9-11, A.S.V.).

THE EVENT DESCRIBED IN THESE VERSES is commemorated by many churches on Ascension Day.

It is a lamentable fact that comparatively little attention is paid by Christians to Ascension Day and the ascension of Jesus Christ. We make much of Christmas, and the cradle in the manger; of Good Friday, and the cross of shame and glory; of Easter Day, and the empty tomb. But we tend to pass by Ascension Day. This is not just because it falls on a week day, but because we seem to attach a smaller importance to Christ's ascension than to His birth, His death, and His resurrection.

It is a pity that we call it Ascension Day, for the Bible speaks more of the exaltation of Jesus than of His ascension. This is an interesting avenue to explore. The four great events in the saving career of Jesus are described in the Bible both actively and passively, as deeds done both by Jesus and to Jesus. Thus, we are told with reference to His birth, both that He came and that He was sent; with reference to His death, both that He gave Himself and that He was offered;

185

with reference to His resurrection, both that He rose and
that He was raised; with reference to His ascension, both that
He ascended and that He was exalted. If we look more closely, we shall find that in the first two cases, the active phrase is
the commoner; He came and He died. It was His deliberate,
self-determined choice. But in the last two cases, the passive
phrase is more common: He was raised from the tomb and
He was exalted to the throne. It was the Father's act.

This is clear in the passage from which my text is taken.
Jesus Christ emptied Himself; He humbled Himself; He
submitted Himself to death on a cross; but He was exalted.
The humbling was His: the exalting was His Father's.

I. His Exaltation Is Supreme

Two expressions are used in these verses to describe the
exaltation of Jesus. First, He was "highly exalted." The
Greek phrase is but one word, and it is unique here in the
New Testament. It means that He was "superexalted," beyond all other exalted things and persons. The exaltation of
Jesus is not just high, but supreme. The second expression
is that He was given "the name which is above every name."
This verse is commonly misunderstood. The name which
He was given is not the name *Jesus*. He was given this name
before His birth, not after His resurrection. In the Hebrew
Old Testament "the name of the Lord" means the majesty
of His Person. The idea is quite common in the phrase to
"praise the name of the Lord." This does not mean to take
the name *Jehovah* and to praise it, but rather to praise the
majesty of Jehovah. So the supreme name which was given
to Jesus refers to His rank, His title, His dignity, which sur-
passed all other ranks, titles and dignities. His name is, in
fact, "*the* name which is above every name."

Now let us pause to consider this. The name of Jesus is
not just one in a catalogue of the world's great men. The
portrait of Jesus is not just one in the portrait gallery of

famous men. The rank of Jesus is not to be compared with any other rank. He is supreme, unique, unrivaled, peerless. God "raised him from the dead, and set him at his own right hand . . . far above all principality, and power, and might, and dominion, and every name that is named" (Eph. 1:20, 21). To concede condescendingly that Jesus of Nazareth was "a very great man" or even "the greatest man who ever lived" is not enough. Name any name you care to choose, and the name of Jesus is greater. Describe any rank you care to describe, and the rank of Jesus is higher.

II. HIS EXALTATION IS MERITED

You will observe that the text which we are studying begins, *"Wherefore also God highly exalted him."* The exaltation of Jesus was not an arbitrary action. It was not the irrational whim of a divine dictator. It was merited. When Cornelius fell on his knees before Peter and worshiped him, Peter said, "Stand up; I too am a man" (Acts 10:25, 26). When John, overcome with emotion, fell down at the feet of the interpreting angel, the angel said: "You must not do that, I am your fellowservant. . . . worship God!" (Rev. 22: 8, 9). When the inhabitants of Lystra brought oxen and garlands and wanted to offer sacrifice to Paul and Barnabas, the apostles tore their garments in horror and rushed out among the crowd, crying: "Men, why are you doing this? We also are men, of like nature with you" (Acts 14:13-15). But when Thomas fell down at the feet of the risen Jesus and said, "My Lord and my God," Jesus accepted his worship. And when all creatures prostrate themselves before His majesty, He does not repudiate their adoration. It is His right. His rank is merited.

Jesus Christ has many titles to this supreme exaltation. I cannot elaborate upon them all, but one of the great themes of the Bible is the superiority of Jesus Christ. The author of the Epistle to the Hebrews demonstrates that He is superior to prophets, angels, Moses, Aaron, and Melchisedec, because He is the Son of God. In the Epistle to the Colossians the supremacy of Christ is linked with the creation. He is described as the only agent of God's old material creation—the universe—and of His new spiritual creation—the Church. Is He "the first born of all creation"? Then "he is before all things." Is He "the firstborn from the dead"? Then He is "the head of the body, the church . . . that in everything he might be pre-eminent" (Col. 1:15-20). In the Epistle to the Philippians it is His work in redemption which entitles Him to exaltation. He humbled Himself. Therefore He was exalted. This is a great spiritual principle stated by Jesus (Luke 14:11; 18:14), by Peter (I Peter 5:6), and by James (4:10). The same principle was illustrated in His life.

He humbled Himself. It began in His mind. Although He was in the form of God, He did not regard His equality with God a prize to be grasped. He emptied Himself. He took the form of a servant. He humbled Himself and became obedient to death on a cross. *Think what He sacrificed!* He left His home and His Father; He left the hymns of worshiping angels; He left the purity of the celestial city; He left the glory which He had before the world was. *Think what He suffered!* He endured poverty and hardship, loneliness and misunderstanding, scorn and rejection, the stinging whip and the crown of thorns, and the desolate agony of the cross. *Think what He achieved!* He secured salvation, perfect and eternal, for all who will come to Him and claim it for themselves. Did He sacrifice and suffer and achieve so much? *"Wherefore* also God highly exalted him." His exaltation corresponds to His humiliation. He humbled Himself to the deepest depths of shame. God has exalted Him to the highest heights of glory.

III. His Exaltation Is Demanding

The text before us contains a statement: "God has highly

exalted him"; a reason: "therefore"; and an application: "in order that. . . ." The exaltation of Jesus was not purposeless, any more than it was arbitrary. God had good cause to exalt Jesus. He also had a clear purpose. This is where we come in. God gave Jesus "the name which is above every name," not only because Jesus deserved it, but also in order that we might recognize it. God has exalted Him that "every knee should bow . . . and every tongue should confess that Jesus Christ is Lord."

This divine demand has little to do with the bending of the knee in a formal genuflection, or with the confession of the tongue in a formal creed. God is not particularly nor primarily interested in the muscular flexibility of our knees and tongues. He is more concerned with the will behind the knee, and with the heart behind the tongue. He wants our bowed knee to betoken the bending of our proud will in homage to Him. He wants our loosened tongue to betoken the warming of our cold heart.

To bow the knee is to do homage to a king. Have we ever done it? We are stiff-necked, stiff-kneed creatures. Let us bow down before Him! He learned obedience; we must learn it too. Disobedience is unbecoming in the child of God.

Whereas the bowing of the knee may be but a private homage, confession with the tongue is a public acclamation. Whether addressed to God in worship or to men in witness, this is the open unashamed confession that Jesus Christ is Lord.

There is no exception to this demand. There is no exemption from this duty. "Every knee" is to bow, and "every tongue" is to confess Christ, "in heaven, on earth and under the earth." That is to say, angels, human beings, and spirits are to unite. The inhabitants of Heaven and earth and Hell are included. Perhaps the most remarkable thing of all about this verse is that it is a quotation from Isaiah 45:22, 23, where the eternal God says: "Turn to me and be saved, all the ends of the earth! For I am God, there is no other . . . to me every knee shall bow, every tongue shall swear." This universal homage which God demands for Himself He now demands for Jesus whom He has exalted to His own right hand.

Here is a message for *one who has never come to Jesus Christ*. Are you resisting His call, wanting to run your own life, to paddle your own canoe, to be king of your own castle? God has exalted Jesus to be supreme. One day you will have to acknowledge His supremacy, for we shall all stand before the judgment seat of Christ, for it is written, "As I live, says the Lord, every knee shall bow to me, and every tongue shall give praise to God" (Rom. 14:10, 11). Why not do voluntarily now what you will one day be compelled to do?

Here also is a message for *one who has hesitations about the rightness of foreign missionary endeavor*. You say perhaps, "Why shouldn't knees bow down to idols and tongues confess other gods?" Such a question is an insult to Jesus Christ. The answer is that God has exalted Him, so that every knee and every tongue should acknowledge *Him,* and no one else.

Here, third, is a message for *the Christian.* How bent is our knee to Christ? How loose is our tongue? Is bending our knee but a momentary curtsy? Is the loosening of our tongue but a diffident stammer? Let us bend our knee lower and open our mouth wider. Let us be more wholehearted in our obedience and more courageous in our witness. He is worthy of more. God desires it. Jesus deserves it. So we must give it. If we do so without reserve, we shall do so without regret.